6-27

UNDERCURRENTS

UNDERCURRENTS

A Therapist's Reckoning with Her Own Depression

MARTHA MANNING

HarperSanFrancisco
A Division of HarperCollins*Publishers*

Permissions can be found on page 201, which constitutes a continuation of this copyright page.

The events described in this book are true. All names and identifying characteristics of patients, doctors, and others have been changed, with the exception of family, friends, and Doctors Bigelow, Jamison, and Waletzky. Many of the entry dates have been altered to allow for the continuity of the story.

FIRST EDITION

Library of Congress Cataloging-in-Publication Data
Manning, Martha.
Undercurrents : a therapist's reckoning with depression / Martha Manning. — 1st ed.
p.   cm.
ISBN 0–06–251183–1 (cloth: alk. paper)
ISBN 0–06–251184–X (pbk.: alk. paper)
1. Manning, Martha—Mental health.   2. Depressed persons—United States—Biography.   3. Psychotherapists—United States—Biography. I. Title.
RC537.M354   1995
616.85′27′0092—dc20   94–33043
[B]

94 95 96 97 98 ❖ HAD 10 9 8 7 6 5 4 3 2 1

This edition is printed on acid-free paper that meets the American National Standards Institute Z39.48 Standard.

for
my husband
Brian Joseph Depenbrock
and
my daughter
Keara Manning Depenbrock

1

Ring the bells that still can ring.
Forget your perfect offering.
There is a crack in everything.
That's how the light gets in.

Leonard Cohen, "Anthem"

January 5, 1990

My nine-year-old patient Stephanie and I sit on the floor of my office playing Sorry. Sorry is one of those wonderful games that is easy even for young children to master, but often difficult for the most mature of adults to tolerate. You can be so close to Home, and be bumped so precipitously by your opponent all the way back to Start. Positions shift quickly. The sure winner loses and the loser triumphs.

Stephanie whoops loudly as she beats me for the third time. Each time she bumps one of my pieces back to Start, she croons "Sooorrryyy" with considerably more delight than remorse. I glance at the clock and let her know that we are close to being out of time. We pack up the box and she places it back on the shelf. I stand up. Without warning, my slip drops to the floor and lands on my shoes. We both stare at it, stunned. I stammer, "Oh my goodness!"

Stephanie, a rather solemn child, is seized with paroxysms of laughter, which become contagious. I step out of my slip and stuff it into my briefcase. Stephanie tries to catch her breath and exclaims, "My perfect Dr. Manning is coming apart!"

She bursts into the crowded waiting room and graphically describes the scene to her parents. It is clear that the entire waiting room enjoys this story. I can see them smiling and smirking behind their *Ladies Home Journals* and *National Geographics*. My friend Ed passes me in the hall between our offices and asks casually, "That wouldn't be your Freudian slip, would it?"

January 8, 1990

My desk is littered with too many things that are getting too little attention. Papers wait passively in the "to do" pile. They've been there so long they are beginning to discolor. Four Diet Coke bottles sit half-filled with warm flat brown liquid. A crusty coffee cup holds the remnants of old candy bars, abandoned midway in fits of guilt. The phone bill is two months overdue and three Medicare forms are screaming for attention. I've been so busy lately, I've started a "to read" pile for the mail I have yet to open. Each evening I leave the office with the magical thought that the night will bring order to the chaos and transform it all by morning. But that is like shoving the box of aluminum foil back into the haphazardly organized closet and closing the door quickly, before it can slide back out. I always hope that time will somehow settle the contents of the closet, and I'm always surprised the next time I open the door when the package slides right back out and smacks me in the head.

I picture a woman who has it all together. She processes things completely the first time they cross her desk. She is up-to-date with bills, Pap smears, and teeth cleanings. She knows that her children's drawers are filled with clean, folded clothes. She knows what her family will be having for dinner three days in advance. She is complete. Able to go to sleep each night without the weight of any old business on the agenda. Everything on her list is crossed off. I hate her.

January 9, 1990

I am on a blitz. A week ago I heard about the National Institutes of Health offering grants for beginning researchers. Since then, it has been constant and frenetic activity: liaison with the grants office, designing the study, estimating budgets, getting endorsements, consultations, statistical input. I'm on my second day of no sleep and I actually feel great. I'm running on fumes with the nutritional support of Diet Coke, coffee, and Hostess powdered-sugar doughnuts. In the middle of the night, hunched over my computer, with the rest of the house dark and quiet, I feel a certain moral superiority to the sleeping world. Even with all this effort, I'm not sure the proposal will be finished by the deadline. But my foot is on the accelerator and I plan to push it to the floor. That's never failed me yet.

January 12, 1990

The grant proposal gets in, with three minutes to spare before the 5:00 P.M. deadline. The department chair dispatches a lab assistant to hand-deliver it to NIH. As we madly collate and staple, I notice a typo and almost start to cry. But it is too late for changes. I whip off a cover letter, pack the damn thing, and send the lab assistant on his mission, encouraging him to consider all speed limits and stoplights as suggested guidelines rather than rigid driving rules. He promises to call me the minute the package is stamped "Received."

For the next hour I put in my time as academic adviser to the parade of students outside my office. I jump when the phone rings. The lab assistant tells me he got it in just under the wire. I thank him profusely and promise that I will never push a proposal to the limit like that again. Before the words fully leave my mouth, I'm aware that I am lying.

January 14, 1990

There is something about flying through time, as I have over the past week, that makes me think that I am exempted from the laws of gravity. But the way I feel today lets me know that I'm not. I have done another of the crash-and-burns that are the price for my blitzes. I am grounded, heavy, and slow. I have overdosed on effort, and the hangover is horrible. I guess this is what I get for flying too close to the sun. Unfortunately, I never remember this part when I am aloft.

January 18, 1990

The house is filthy. Every pile is a testament to good intentions gone nowhere. Dark green garbage bags line the wall of the living room—old clothes to be taken to the Salvation Army. They've been there so long, we've started leaving our coats and backpacks on them like they are innovative pieces of furniture. The county is going to be able to make a major addition to its budget with the overdue fines on the pile of library books by the door. Old potatoes are doing despicable things in the broom closet, and what really worries me is that we're getting used to the smell.

I'd rather buy new underwear than tackle the mountain of laundry molding in the basement. I'm wearing a pair of

Brian's briefs. Not even the designer kind with interesting colors and cuts, just the plain white Fruit of the Looms. I'm worried that I'll be in a car accident and people in the emergency room will think I'm a cross-dresser. Yesterday all that was left in my underwear drawer was this little black thing from Victoria's Secret that was clearly meant to remain on the body for no more than ten minutes. All through student advising, a three-hour lecture on statistical reliability, and interviews with prospective graduate students, I was constantly aware of the presence of my underwear. I felt like I had a permanent wedgie. The Fruit of the Looms today are a vast improvement.

Over the years, Brian and I have been true to our pledge to share the household tasks. Lately, however, that means that we do equal amounts of nothing. My well-organized friend Pat once told me that she almost bought me an apron that said, "The only domestic thing about me is that I live in a house." She thought it was wildly funny. At best, I found it only mildly amusing. I want to be domestic. I want to be one of those women who, after working long days, come home and fix nutritious, interesting meals for their families. I want to have bathrooms that are clean enough so that when people drop by unexpectedly, I don't have to worry that they might have to pee. I want to have a refrigerator that doesn't look like I'm working on a replacement for penicillin. I want to make a pie crust that doesn't stick to the counter. But I just don't seem to be able to pull it off. And things are getting worse.

I rush out of a late faculty meeting, pick up the cleaning, drop off the videos, and collect Keara from play practice. I ask that special question that always goes over much better on television than it does in my car: "How about McDonald's?"

Keara turns up her nose and counts off the number of times we've had fast food in the past week. She's learning about nutrition in school and asks sanctimoniously, "Do you know how many fat grams there are in a Big Mac?" like I just asked her to eat dirt. Keara sighs and says, "I wish you'd make home-cooked dinners like you used to."

"Like what?" I remember only my alternating baked chicken and meat loaf.

"Like remember how you used to always make that Kraft macaroni and cheese and those Spaghetti Os?"

Things are really bad. Boxed and canned prepared foods constitute my kid's culinary good old days. We are sorely in need of professional help.

The idea of having someone come in to clean disturbs me. It's a moral dictate: you messed it up, you clean it up. There is also the embarrassment factor. I am mortified at the thought of a stranger seeing not only the outside visible mess, but the dirt and disorder in all those secret places: the linen closet, the refrigerator vegetable drawers, under the beds, behind the couches.

I remind myself that all my friends have had cleaning help for years. It's come down to choices: quit my volunteer work or have a clean house, stop trying to write so many grant proposals or have a clean house, stop driving Keara all over the county or have a clean house.

My friend Pat recommends Sima, the woman who cleans her house. When I call her she is glad for the work but sounds disappointed when I tell her that I don't live in Pat's neighborhood, which is considerably more upscale than mine. We come to an agreement on duties, time, and price, and I feel decidedly better, like I actually might get control over my own household again.

Sima comes on Friday morning. She is dropped off by her husband, who, she tells me immediately, treats her badly. For five minutes we stand by the front door as she fills me in on the difficulties of her life and the ways in which her different employers are helpful to her. I wonder if she is articulating some unspoken part of the contract, and I swallow hard thinking about how much I need one more person in my life who expects help from me. I try to move things along so that I can leave for work, and suggest that we tour the house. As we walk around, she alternates between telling me how lovely my friends' houses are and making clucking and tsking sounds as she checks out various rooms. She asks questions like, "When was the last time you washed the windows?" with a certain tone of disgust like she smells something bad and is asking, "When was the last time you bathed?" When we finish the tour, she declares, "You really need me. This is going to take a lot of work." I ask what she means and she answers, "Your house may be much smaller than Pat's, but it's so much dirtier." She increases the price she quoted me on the phone because things "are a lot worse" than she expected. I am totally and completely ashamed of myself. Somehow, in the space of a half hour I feel myself moving from an employer paying for a straightforward service to a supplicant offering anything for deliverance from my domestic negligence. Within only a few minutes, Sima gains the upper hand. And I have no idea how to get it back.

January 19, 1990

I hand out an exam to my first-year doctoral students in Psychological Assessment. We're so pressed for lecture time that I make it a take-home exam. The students look terrible, too much work on too little sleep in this academic hell we call "the first year of graduate school." They sigh as they pass the exams around, handling them like they weigh several pounds rather than several ounces.

I always feel slightly sadistic at times like these. But damn it, they've got to master this material or they're going to pay later on. All rationalization, but it helps me tolerate their barrage of questions containing a mixture of anxiety and hostility.

I love teaching. It is one of the few things in my life that feels more like a mission than a job. Training doctoral students has a way of keeping me honest in my own work. It stretches me, makes me reach. Teaching a doctoral seminar helps me on a weekly basis to realize that despite my obsessive notes, references, and lists, my ignorance is still so much greater than my knowledge. I think that is probably applicable to every academic field, but so acutely true in the work of a clinical psychologist. Despite the burgeoning technologies in the field of "helping," on many levels psychotherapy is still a crapshoot. Some of the goal of training, I think, is to help students accept that fact. The work is part science, part art, and part luck. Learning to tolerate the anxiety inherent in that recipe is critical for any clinician.

I have a way of getting derailed easily in my lectures, letting students' questions lead me down roads that are admittedly scenic, but detour me from ever reaching the final page of my lecture notes. I tell them stories, usually from my clinical experience, sometimes from my own life. These students are on to me. They are now experts at getting me off track. But today, as I feel myself beginning to veer away from the subject at hand, which is not even particularly interesting to me, I stop myself and state categorically, "No, we are going to get through every page of these damn notes today if it kills me. I am not getting off the subject."

There is a collective groan and one student complains, "But Martha, you're at your best when you're off the subject."

I lecture, straight from my notes, no exceptions. It is one of those dark afternoons when the sun checks out too early, leaving people stifling yawns in overheated rooms. The fatigue gradient of doctoral students can be easily plotted by measuring that proportion of body mass that is positioned upright approximately one hour into the cognitive marathons we call graduate seminars. Today the students are practically horizontal to the table. Nevertheless, I make great headway through my notes, and I am exceedingly pleased with myself.

Finally, a student cries out for mercy, begging to be delivered from one more correlation coefficient or factor analysis. She blurts out, "Martha, *please,* tell us some stories." I feel like the doctor who holds the shot behind her back, hoping to hell that the poor kid will somehow know that the pain coming is for his own good. I strike a deal with them—five more pages of my notes, and then I will tell them some "stories." They sit straighter in their chairs, now reassured that this unappealing dinner will soon be followed by dessert.

January 23, 1990

As I tuck Keara in, she asks if I will take her to the Gap tomorrow for a pair of jeans. When I agree, she sighs with great contentment. She sinks back into her pillows and turns to me like she's going to indulge me in some major personal disclosure.

"Mom, you know how you're always writing in your head?" she asks.

"Yeah, honey, I know," I answer.

"Well," she says proudly, "I'm always shopping in mine."

January 24, 1990

I take Keara shopping, which is my idea of purgatory on earth. I'm sure that I get time off for good behavior every time I enter a store with that child. I try on two large, dark, baggy turtlenecks at the Gap. They look like hell on me, but they are cotton, warm and comfortable. And these days, in clothes selection, I don't care about much else. Keara surveys the racks like we're in a museum and she is contemplating great art. I choose my turtlenecks in two minutes. She chooses her jeans in two hours.

February 3, 1990

On the spur of the moment on a mercifully empty Saturday morning, Brian and I play racquetball. I love it when he agrees to play me. I am no match for his power, but I'm fast, which makes things a bit more equitable. Nevertheless, he beats me about six games to one. There is something so primal, so basic about sweating it out on the court, trying to beat the pants off him. Diving into him to get a shot, bumping up against him as we trade places for a serve, hitting, huffing, sweating, swearing. Sex with racquets.

Brian tells me that I "have a lot of energy," which is his way of saying that I'm all over the court. He holds back the strength of his serves for me until about halfway through the hour, when I tell him, "Give me all you've got." He slams that sucker and it whizzes past my head like a guided missile. It takes me a while, but I get the rhythm of it, very different from the games I play with my friend Ginger during the week.

When the buzzer rings at the end of the hour, I am secretly grateful because I am exhausted, although I would never admit it to him. We retire to our respective locker rooms. "High-level aerobics" has just let out, and I am condemned to showering and changing with a bunch of twenty-three-year-olds who don't have a wrinkle on their faces or their thighs. They parade naked around the room, frowning as they weigh themselves and moaning to friends that they still can't get those three pounds off. I love to look at the scale when a thin woman gets off. Thin women have an arrogance about the etiquette of locker-room weighing. Rather than slide the weight back to zero, they leave the marker right where it landed, usually in the 105 to 110 range. On kinder days I dismiss it as an oversight in the hurry to get dressed. On my darker days, however, I'm sure it is a silent statement of superiority, left behind for the next poor woman to beat. I am fascinated by these women. Every now and then, I see someone who meets my fantasy of what I would someday like to look like. I want to approach her and say, "Could you tell me *exactly* what you eat, *exactly* what you do for exercise, and, if I do it all perfectly, can I look *exactly* like you?"

I meet Brian downstairs and we agree to hit the local diner for breakfast. It is unusual to be able to make impromptu plans like this, but Keara will be at her sleep-over till noon, so we have plenty of time. He rolls back the sunroof, even though it can't be more than forty degrees out, and blasts the radio as we cruise down the road. Aretha Franklin is demanding "Respect" and Brian and I oblige her in the chorus. We belt out "sock it to me, sock it to me . . . " all eight times, greatly pleased that we can still sing it all in one breath. For a moment I forget that we are solidly in our thirties, driving a sensible gray station wagon, balding and spreading, responsible and serious and tired, navigating the same old roads that seem to go nowhere. Suddenly, we are once again in our teens, flying around in his fire-engine-red '68 Chevy Impala convertible. We are intoxicated by the wind, lifted by the music, and soaring at the thought of the wide-open road before us. I'm a little sorry when we slow down at the turn for the diner. I could drive with him like this all day.

Sammy's Diner is packed. It's not one of those upscale replicas of 1950s diners. This place is the real thing. The jukebox shouts with an alternating mix of heavy metal and country music, which keeps me constantly off balance. The manic cook at the grill bellows "PICK UP!" every few seconds as he slams his completed orders on the bar. We slide into the only available booth, which is located right next to the jukebox. Faded Dallas Cowboys photos cover the wall, a heroic and heretical statement in Redskin-crazy Washington.

Sammy's is a great melting pot. Two gay men who are making no secret of their affection for each another sit across from a group of tattooed, leathered bikers who keep their sunglasses on while they eat. Three silver-haired ladies in polyester pantsuits are across from them, sipping coffee and discussing their husbands' prostate problems. A family who look like they just stepped out of an L. L. Bean catalog sample each other's food at the table in the corner. The only thing Brian doesn't like about eating out with me is that I love to watch other people and eavesdrop on their conversations. When he frowns, I insist that he should understand, since as therapists we both make our living from being professional voyeurs. The menus arrive and I reluctantly turn my attention away from the action.

The menu at Sammy's is a personal invitation to obesity, cancer, and heart disease. But no one looks the least bit concerned. I order a breakfast that will taste great while I'm eating it, and horrible in two hours. I rationalize the choice of fried eggs, potatoes, and sausage with the fact that I just played an hour of racquetball. If I were honest with myself and actually did the math, I'd see that it would take about twelve hours on the courts to work off what I'm shoveling into my mouth right now.

There is a momentary and welcome pause in the music. A woman in a short green dress that has to be at least three sizes too small for her studies the jukebox. I notice that she is talking to herself, but dismiss it, figuring that she is just reading aloud from the list of titles. I am pleased when she chooses "Fast Car," a haunting tune by Tracy Chapman. But then she pulls out a musical triangle from her purse and begins to play it and sing along with the record. She has a wobbly high voice that clashes with the dusky deep one on the jukebox. The clatter of the diner quiets as everyone begins to take notice. She is right next to our table as she gives the performance of a lifetime. With all eyes aimed in our direction, Brian and I do our best to keep our eyes on our plates, knowing that if we look at her or each other, we will explode in laughter. I always feel bad laughing at people who act crazy. But sometimes the things they do are so damned funny. I wonder what I'd look like if I slipped a few notches on the mental-health index. With my predilection for singing and dancing to loud rocking music, I'd probably be right up there with her. I give Brian permission to shoot me if I ever go that far off the deep end. I'm a bit dismayed at how quickly he agrees.

February 4, 1990

Whoever said that the Sabbath was a day of rest was a fool. Unless, of course, it was God or Christ or somebody, and then I take it back. But it is Sunday afternoon and I'm exhausted. I'm becoming an overachiever at church.

We sleep through the alarm. I'm in the middle of a sexy dream when Brian's knee bumps my ass as he scrambles out of bed yelling, "Holy shit, we're late for church." We drag Keara out of bed, assess the damage, and decide there's no time to shower or eat. The best we can do is brush our teeth and throw on clothes. I can't find my plans for the Sunday school class I'm teaching later and curse my head off about "the people in this family who move my stuff." We race out the door. Brian asks if I've had a chance to look in the mirror. When I say no, Keara laughs and tells me I have a bad case of "bed head." I look and see that some of my very short hair is sticking straight up, giving me a look that could be stylish and trendy on someone twenty years younger, but on me just looks slobby and stupid. There's no time to wash my hair, so I take a lot of heavy-duty hair spray, hold down the offending pieces, and spray the hell out of them until they stay still.

We are late for choir practice and grab pieces of coffee cake on the way in. They are already practicing a new song, which is unfortunate since I can't read music and realize I will just have to sit next to one of the serious singers and fake it. I don't belong in the choir. I have a lousy voice. But I love the choir director, a fantastically talented man whose voice makes me want to stand up and sing alleluia, something that rarely happens for me in church. Between songs I surreptitiously devour pieces of coffee cake and wonder whether I'll have time after practice to find a soda machine so I can get in my two hits of Diet Coke before mass begins.

I know I'm forgetting something. I see Maria, the liturgy coordinator, in the hall and she checks in to make sure I have written the litany of prayers that comes after the sermon. I try to look like I wrote them weeks ago and tell her, "Oh yeah, I'm ready." I rush to my seat with the choir and rummage around in my backpack for paper and pencil so that I can do a blitz on the prayers. My backpack is so loaded with trash that the best piece of paper I can find is a grocery store receipt. Luckily it was for over two hundred dollars, so I have some space. How am I going to stand up on that altar and read prayers from a roll of grocery tape? While the priest introduces himself, I search for a pen as quietly as possible. Brian looks over at me from the bass section with one of his "What the hell are you doing?" expressions. I finally hit on what I think is a pen and pull it out to use, only to find that it is really a pink, plastic-covered tampon. Brian starts to laugh. I throw it back. The only thing that writes is a brown crayon, which will have to do. I write some prayers, inviting the congregation to pray for world peace, an end to hatred and hunger, the usual stuff. We are a quarter of the way through the service and I have yet to register a word of what is going on in the mass. When I finish with the prayers I realize that I have to plan my Sunday school class, which meets immediately afterward. So I start to obsess about that, berating myself for being so disorganized.

We stand for the reading of the Gospel. It is a priest I don't know and he reads the Gospel with life and passion. The story is about Martha and Mary, which always piques my interest because my mother named me for the Martha in this Gospel. She always felt that Martha got a raw deal from Christ, and named me as some sort of protest. Martha and Mary were sisters who, with their brother Lazarus, were close friends of Christ. One day Christ and his friends drop by for a visit. Martha, the organizer, goes into overdrive, hustling to get the place picked up and dinner on the table. The rest of the people gather around Christ, hanging on his every word. Mary is right there at Christ's feet soaking up the entire experience, while Martha is busy, probably wondering how she can stretch left-overs ten ways. Feeling the burdens of too much work and not enough help finally gets to her. Given the sexism of the times, she is particularly irked with Mary for hanging out with the guys instead of attending to all the tasks of hospitality. She finally bitches to Christ, righteously demanding that he tell Mary to get off her ass and help out. Christ looks at her and delivers a pronouncement that is burned in my memory, since more than one nun in my childhood pulled my hair and repeated these words when I was misbehaving: "Martha, Martha, you are anxious and troubled about many things. . . ." So far, it sounds like he was pretty much on the money, but then he delivers the clincher, the one that puts Martha in her place and really pisses my mother off. "There is need of only one thing. Mary has chosen the better part and it will not be taken from her" (Luke 10:38–42).

My mother, a tremendously practical woman, always held her own sermon after this particular reading as we walked home from church. "Easy for him to say while he was given a place to rest, and the comforts of food and drink. How was all that supposed to materialize if everyone just remained sitting at his feet?"

She challenged the typical church sermons for that reading, which pontificated about the absolute ascendancy of the spiritual over the worldly. My mother always found this a bit ironic, coming from a bunch of men whose daily concerns with such menial tasks as cooking, cleaning, and sewing were consigned to poorly paid housekeepers or to nuns, whose basic vocation in life was to take care of priests for free. While I agreed in principle with my mother on this point, I always wished she hadn't seen fit to take issue with Christ by plastering the name *Martha* (first) *Mary* (second) on the birth certificate of her totally innocent firstborn child.

As the priest begins the sermon, I am prepared once again to be annoyed. I get ready to organize for Sunday school. One minute into this guy's talk and he has my rapt attention. He has a commanding presence and a great facility with language. There is something electric about him. I can't help myself. For once, I put everything aside and just sit there and listen.

He eschews the typical party line and talks about not choosing between Martha and Mary, but integrating both of those aspects within ourselves. He applauds Martha for having her feet firmly planted on the earth, for taking care of business, for being practical and organized. He emphasizes the absolute necessity of these attributes if one is to get through the demands of daily life and effectively translate the word of God into action. The downside, he admits, is getting lost in the details. In being so concerned with the dirty streaks on the windows that you lose the marvel of the sunset, in being so anchored in the body that you lose hold of the soul. Still gripping my brown crayon, I have an experience I have never had in church. In some kind of benign paranoia, I feel like he is talking directly to me. My face is hot and I am uncomfortable in my seat. The goal, he says, is for each of us to struggle constantly with the Martha and Mary within ourselves, to balance the real and present demands on our time and energy with the need to let go, to reflect and listen, to be always open to the divine.

After mass I do something I have never done before. I go up to him to introduce myself. I have no idea why, or what I want to say. There are people around him and I hang back and wait until they leave.

He looks me over and says almost challengingly, "And who are you?"

I answer, "I am Martha Mary."

He grins and takes both my hands, pulling me close to him. He stares me dead in the eyes and asks, "Did you hear what I said?"

I nod and tell him it was very good. But he waves away the compliment. Instead, he squeezes my hands and says, "Someday you will do more than hear. You will understand. And when you do, that message will explode in your head and your life will never be the same again."

I just stand there, staring at him. Other people begin to approach. He kisses my forehead, lightly, almost like a blessing, and says, "Good-bye, Martha Mary."

All I can do is nod. I feel like I have just spent a couple of minutes in the *Twilight Zone*. I have no idea what just happened. I know this absolute stranger has told me something important, but I don't know what it really means. Exactly what is going to "explode in my head"? How will my life "never be the same"? But the question that really bothers me is, when the hell is "someday"?

February 17, 1990

A long, sad day that leaves me weary and confused. Annie comes in for her session. The results of the CAT scan are back and the news is about as bad as it can be. The cause of the killer headaches and possible seizures of last week is now clear.

Despite being in the midst of another round of aggressive chemotherapy, her metastatic breast cancer has now established itself solidly in her brain. She sits there in a bright scarf covering a head that is bald for the second time, her face swollen from steroids, a slight tremor in her hands, and she cries at the news she heard less than an hour ago.

Annie and I are the same age. Her daughter is Keara's age. She came to me a year ago, after her first round of chemotherapy. Like many people who have been through trauma, she found herself confused that she had coped so well through the tests, diagnosis, surgery, and chemotherapy but found herself falling apart just when it was "all over." I am learning in my work with cancer patients that the end of chemotherapy is not the point when it is all over. In some ways it is the point at which things are just beginning.

Annie is the first person with cancer I had ever seen in my practice. I didn't want to take the referral. I wasn't sure whether my skills would extend to an area about which I knew so little, but I read, and I listened, and I learned. And I hoped it would be enough. She struggled with so many of the things people must tackle when they go through something like this: changes in her body and in her self-confidence and image, disruptions in work and family, the loss of innocence that comes from seeing the fragility of your own young life, long before you thought it was time.

Over the year our work has woven in and out of the mundane (how to tolerate the itchy, sweaty breast prosthesis in the summer months) to the existential (the constant sense of living on borrowed time). We watched her hair grow in like the hair that sticks straight up on baby chicks. Every session she would lift her stylish shoulder-length wig to get my assessment of whether she was ready to ditch it. One week, on an unbearably hot day, she scratched and tugged at it during the entire session.

She finally got fed up and sputtered, "The hell with it. I don't care what anyone thinks anymore." She ripped it off and threw it in her purse, smoothing and stroking her own seedlings of hair.

The next week we talked about dealing with people's stares and the cruel remark of some smart-ass kid who sneered at her super-short hair and yelled, "You dyke."

Just when things were looking better, a regular checkup spotted trouble. The cancer had metasticized. Her response to this setback was feisty as hell. She was determined not to give in, declaring that she still had a kid to raise. On the day she got the diagnosis, she brought in a tape of Pete Seeger performing the old Quaker song, "How Can I Keep from Singing?" She played it for me on the boom box I keep in the office. It is a song of strength and transcendence—the lyrics seemed written just for her.

> My life flows on in endless song, above earth's lamentation.
> I hear the real, though far-off humn that hails a new creation.
> No storm can shake my inmost calm, while to that rock I'm clinging.
> Since love is lord of heaven and earth,
> How can I keep from singing?

It became a fight song for her and a sort of code between us. We used it in making relaxation and imagery tapes for her to work with at home. She fought on and on. But then the headaches started. And even in my ignorance, I knew that wasn't good.

Today we sit in silence. Sometimes silence is the "therapeutic" thing to do. But now it is because I have no idea what to say.

She gets out of her chair and paces the length of my office, telling me that her prognosis is impossibly poor and that she has decided not to endure the remaining chemotherapy treatments. Part of me wants to urge her on in the fight, like a cheerleader for a team that is woefully behind in the last five seconds. I don't want her to give up. I want her to try anything, push it to the limit, give it all she's got. But I look at her through eyes that are beginning to water and realize that she's been doing precisely that for over a year now, with drastically diminishing returns.

She walks to her purse and pulls out a pack of cigarettes. Cigarettes that she quit with such reluctance and difficulty after the first diagnosis. She says almost defiantly, "I bought them on the way over. Can I smoke in here?" The hospital building I'm in is so rabidly antismoking that I'm sure the first puff of smoke will set off screaming alarms, so I suggest we go outside. We lean against a green Buick as she lights up and takes her first drag with immense satisfaction. Our faces are raised to the sun, which is sneaking in an appearance, teasing us with a promise of spring. She tells me that her priest, Father Steve, is coming over to anoint her and that she plans to continue attending the healing services at her church. I nod. Outside the office, leaning against a car, it seems that some of the boundaries that separate patient from therapist evaporate. She nudges me with her elbow and protests, "Don't just nod. Tell me what you believe."

With my typical psychologist's deflection, I respond, "It's what *you* believe that's more important."

"Don't give me that shrink crap right now. I need for you to talk to me," she protests.

"Well," I begin, "there is some interesting research that supports the potential healing power of prayer. The operative variables in it are not clear, but . . . "

She becomes irritated and breaks in, "Martha, that's what you read. What do you *believe?*"

I am caught so short, I almost lose my breath. "Believe about what?" I ask.

"About God answering our prayers, about what happens when we die."

And I, who pride myself on being able to use language to bullshit my way out of any number of awkward situations, can't find a word to say. I want to speak. But I owe this woman so much more than bullshit. I figure that all I can give her is honesty, so I admit that I really don't know. I want to know. At times I've thought I've known. But right now, I just don't know. She seems satisfied with this woeful response. She tells me that she, herself, isn't totally sure, but that she is trying hard to believe in a God who still hears her, even if that God will not heal her in the way she is asking.

As if sensing my discomfort with her questions, she grabs my hand and asks, "You're gonna stay with me, right?"

"Stay with you?" I repeat.

"Until the end." she replies.

The end. We let those words settle deep into the silence between us. I squeeze her hand and finally the words come from someplace inside me other than my head.

"Yeah, Annie, I'm gonna stay with you."

She sighs and lights up again, offering me the pack. I'm not a smoker, but in that moment I wish like hell I was.

February 18, 1990

For my father's seventieth birthday we decide to play the television game show *Jeopardy,* with his life divided into the different categories. My sister Priscilla is assigned to get background information from his sisters and friends for questions on his early life. Brian is appointed to play host Alex Trebek and my brother Chip, his sidekick announcer Johnny Gilbert. The "outlaws," Ann, Greg, and Darrell, are assigned to be contestants. I volunteer to design the game board, and all six of us agree to come up with questions and gag prizes for the "double" rounds.

I watch *Jeopardy* and take copious notes. We sweep through a hobby shop, buying huge thick blue poster board, scissors, glue, Magic Markers, and a lot of little junky things like stars, stickers, and glitter that might spice it up. I feel like a little kid until Brian puts the brakes on before I have a complete arts-and-crafts attack. I start working on the board at 9:00 P.M., thinking I can knock it off in an hour. But fifteen minutes into it I'm a goner. I keep having inspirations about how to make it even better. I get really obsessive, torturously applying hundreds of stick-on numbers and letters, playing with different fonts on the computer for the best titles, and making fifty tiny question holders out of envelopes. I call it "John Manning Jeopardy" and go to town with the stars and glitter. Unlike its real-life counterpart, which is fairly straightforward and conservative, this game board is glitzy and gaudy, looking like it should be in Las Vegas with a craps table under it. My back is killing me, my head hurts from squinting at all the tiny letters, and I'm exhausted. This makes sense when I see that the clock registers 3:30 A.M. I can't stop admiring it, even though I am painfully aware of the price I will pay for all this tomorrow.

We gather at my sister Rachel's an hour before my parents are due to arrive and do our usual blitz putting things together. Sometimes the collective energy of the six siblings disintegrates quickly into tension and fragmentation. Tonight, however, we

2

I measure every grief I meet
        with analytic eyes;
I wonder if it weighs like mine,
        Or has an easier size.

I wonder if they bore it long,
        Or did it just begin?
I could not tell the date of mine,
        It feels so old a pain.

I wonder if it hurts to live,
        And if they have to try,
And whether could they choose between,
        They would not rather die.

Emily Dickinson

June 16, 1990

I feel like my old Ford Escort when the transmission started slipping. Transmissions don't just break down all at once. The process is more insidious, with total collapse threatening at every shift, every change. The transitions get harder and harder. The car balks, then chokes, and finally almost seems to groan as I put my hand on the gearshift and ask it to do something more than cruise on automatic. I can almost feel the effort, the pulling out of all the stops just to cover distance that was accomplished before with a simple tap on the gas.

My own transmission is slipping. What was once so smooth, so automatic, is now forced and effortful and unpredictable. The key to fixing myself should be so simple, so obvious that I will kick myself when I finally realize it. When I took my driver's exam I tried so hard to manage the anxiety and the clutch simultaneously, but the car sputtered and hesitated and kept giving out within the first three minutes of the road test. The guy doing the test was a sadistic son of a bitch who just kept shaking his head and writing on his blasted clipboard. Finally he sighed loudly and said patronizingly, "Miss Manning, do you realize that you are trying to drive with the parking brake on?" I quickly released it, relieved to know what the problem was, and I started to drive again. But he growled, "Pull over. The test is terminated." He flunked me and told me to come back in two weeks. I found out what the problem was, but it was too late.

I don't need anyone to tell me now that I'm trying to drive with the parking brake on. I can feel it. But this time I don't know how to release it. I'm afraid I'm going to fail again. And this time it feels like an exam with no second chances.

After a week of back-and-forth ambivalence, I give my old therapist, Jeremy Waletzky, a call. He is technically on sab-

are pure synergy. Everyone is funny and we play off one another like a bunch of stand-up comedians. We rig up the board behind a sliding glass door with full-length drapes that can be pulled back in a dramatic surprise. Brian and Chip practice their announcer voices. People share information about my father gained from their various contacts. I am sorry he is missing this part, because I can't imagine that the real thing could be any funnier.

The game is hysterical. The questions routinely stump the "outlaws" and often leave even my father guessing. Intermittently, the contestants hit on the "daily double" categories with prizes attached. One is a "deluxe array of delicious pastries, perfectly sized for stashing, hiding, and hoarding." It is actually a collection of the junkiest of the junk snack cakes—pink marshmallow and coconut chocolate cream-filled cupcakes, Little Debbies, Ho-Ho's, Mallomars. Great for throwing into the trunk of his Volvo and hiding from the watchful, more nutrition-conscious eyes of my mother.

My father alternates between laughing uproariously and getting choked up and teary-eyed. This man is so much more real to me at seventy than he was at thirty-five. Then he was a stranger—a hard-hitting FBI agent who left for the city early in the morning and didn't return until after dinners and homeworks and baths. He began running before it was popular, when the only reason a man would run on the street was because he was late or being chased. Now, though still intense, he is right here, with time for everyone. He remains in constant motion, currently alternating between organizing his Marine Corps reunion and preparing for the upcoming Barbie convention, where collectors of Barbie dolls (who could ever believe it) come to view displays of Barbies dressed up in Shakespearian tableaux or attend seminars on issues like "The History of

Skipper." And what I love so much is that he couldn't give a damn about the seeming inconsistency of it all.

The game ends. My father laughs, collects all the little question cards that have been discarded around the room, picks up the gag prizes, and tells us, "This was great, kids, just great," promising to put up the board in his study. My brothers and sisters and I are delighted with our ingenuity. It is pure pleasure to give something to someone you love and have it received with such joy.

February 26, 1990

My mother calls this morning, frustrated with dealing with my grandmother long distance. Grandmother is eighty-eight years old—still young as women in my family go—but she is less and less able to cope. Her children wonder how much longer, despite her insistence, she can stay in that huge house alone. My mother struggles aloud to understand my grandmother, something she has been trying to do her entire life. She doesn't understand the weariness, the passivity, the cutting-to-the-quick anger. The rage so smoldering beneath the surface of her relationships that you always fear coming too close, talking too long, because it could be that one look, that one word, that turns the rumbling to a roar. I know what my mother is describing. It is etched in my mind, as a memory and a warning.

The memory is so clear because it has happened so many times:

My grandmother sits at the kitchen table. The table is technically clean, but always sticky. A lazy Susan spins in the center, with the host of prescription bottles, holy cards of dead people, Avon products, and napkins. Round and round; I watch

as the salt and pepper are replaced in my sight by the sugar.
I watch the objects move as I circle my grandmother's depression.
I pray that Brian and Keara will remain at the table, that they
will keep her amused and, in so doing, camouflage the real
action. Their funny stories and their hugging affection bubble
along the surface. And they are tolerated, even remotely enjoyed
by my grandmother. They are allowed into the first level, the one
that shows a contrived but happy face to the world. But her real
faces are on other levels. They are in her arms resting wearily
against the table, in a jumper and blouse that have to be the
worst-looking things even in a poor woman's closet, in the weight
of my grandfather's heavy gold watch clinking against her teacup.

I don't want them to leave me alone with her, as they
always end up doing. Despite my pleadings, despite the looks that
greet their impatience and motion for them to sit back down,
despite the clenching of my teeth and jaw that shows I mean
business. Despite the warnings, they fall off to some other room
and leave me with the inevitable showdown.

I sit and feel the backs of my thighs digging into the chair.
I bear down so hard I can feel the ridges in the seat making
indentations in my ass. My knees are tight, my toes are curled. I
brace myself for it. And she sighs. She exhales in a way that
screams, "I give up. I am already dead." And I worry that she
somehow has the power to take me with her. "It's only a sigh,"
Brian says to me. But then she leans over and says, "Oh
Maaaaaaathaaaaaa." It's never more than that. It doesn't have to
be. In that lament is the absolute and total conveyance of sorrow.
And I know it is my cue to urge her on in her litany of pain, back
and forth, like a priest and an acolyte.

Other people deal with it better than I. They have more
distance. Her sorrow is not separate from me. It is in me too. I
know it. I've known it all along. I have lived all my life with

parallel visions of her: my magical creative wonderful grandmother who calls me golden and loves me like crazy, and the sad, angry woman who gave up on life so long ago.

The affinity I feel with her must be fought. I must break free and struggle to the surface where I can breathe and have a life that calls from me the happy, the joyous, rather than the resounding despair she sings to me. She emits a frequency that can only be received by like beings. I register with precision the timbre of her discontent. I smell the storm brewing before the rest of the world even notices the clouds.

March 5, 1990

My annual gynecological checkup. I drive twenty-five minutes to my friend Rob's office, which I wouldn't do for any other doctor. He has seen me through two miscarriages with a care and gentleness that I assumed was trained out of most physicians in medical school. The waiting room is packed, filled with pregnant women who form an instant club, united in their fecundity. They chat like intimates and I am the stranger. One of my patients who recently suffered a miscarriage complained to me that an OB-GYN's waiting room should have two sections, like pediatricians have for "sick" and "well" children: pregnant and nonpregnant. There is a certain torture to sitting in a roomful of round satisfied women. It makes me experience an emptiness that the rest of my busy life helps me forget. I bury myself in a copy of *Good Housekeeping* and learn about a woman who has elevated coupon-clipping to a science and spends about thirty-eight cents on a week's worth of groceries.

Finally the nurse calls me in to go over the usual medical history. She notes my proximity to forty, and all of a sudden I'm into a whole new genre of questions, the worst one being: "Have you started losing bladder control yet?"

I get flustered and reply with alarm, "Am I supposed to?"

She tries to be reassuring and answers, "Oh no, it's just that some women your age begin experiencing it."

Women my age? What does that mean? I flash to future scenes of myself walking down grocery store aisles with those large packages of Depends undergarments in my cart, recalling how many years it took me to get comfortable paying for Tampax in a checkout line.

Next comes the dreaded weigh-in. I step on the scale like I'm going to my death and stand there while she adjusts the balance. She is extremely generous in her initial assessment of my weight and expresses surprise as she inches the balance farther and farther to the right. In dismay she complains, "I'm usually great at estimating. Do you have rocks in your pockets?" She finally strikes the balance on the scale and shakes her head as she fills in the number on my chart. I don't know why, but I feel the need to reassure her about her capabilities. "Don't worry," I tell her, "It happens all the time. I must be dense."

With that torture completed, I am left to don the requisite blue print gown, which essentially covers nothing but gives the illusion that you're retaining some shred of decency. There is something about taking off my regular I-live-and-function-in-the-world clothes and putting on one of these skimpy outfits that always brings me down a few notches in the self-confidence department.

There's no way to sit on the examining table in these getups with any grace or stature. In the time to kill while waiting for Rob, I notice that in my haste to shave my legs, I missed whole stretches. They are winter white, with a dry, chapped cast that makes the dark hairs stand out even more than usual. The patchy remnants of red polish on my toes are a testimony to making an occasional effort, but never quite following through over the long term. I hear Rob's voice in the hall and then his fiddling with the rack on the door to retrieve my chart.

He bursts in with smiles and open arms. I try to negotiate the hug as best I can in the stupid little gown. We exclaim about how it's been too long since we've seen each other and then get down to business with the exam. As he palpates my breasts, we exchange catch-up information about our spouses, children, and practices, like we're chatting over roast beef sandwiches at lunch. Then he tells me to "scoot down" for the pelvic exam. After the perfunctory warning about the cold speculum, he begins to tell me how tired he is and wonders aloud if he might be a bit depressed. He's up to his elbows inside me as I ask about his symptoms. He tinkers around in my reproductive tract like he's working under the hood of a car, looking up every now and then to emphasize a point about how lousy he feels. His recounting suggests a mild clinical depression. As he inserts the long swab for the Pap smear, he asks me for my clinical impression. I am spread out like an untrussed turkey with this man's head between my legs and he is poised there waiting for my professional advice.

I tell him, "Y'know, Rob, this isn't exactly my best thinking position."

He sits upright, tosses his surgical gloves in the trash, pushes himself back on the stool, and says, "Oh, I'm finished. Everything looks great."

He helps me to get out of the stirrups and into an upright position. I sit there with my hairy legs swung over the edge of the table. He's perched on the stool ready for conversation. There is no way to pull the gown down any farther than I've already got it. I try crossing my legs, which proves to be a big mistake. Then I figure, "What the hell. This guy has plumbed the depths of me on numerous occasions. Who cares about dignity."

We talk about depression, about medicine, about psychotherapy. We talk about the downside of the helping professions: absorbing too much of people's pain, burning out. It is uncomfortable listening to him. What he has the courage to voice out loud is what has been whispering softly in my own mind recently. I just try not to pay it too much attention.

Rob sighs and says that he wishes he could see me as a therapist. This man who has been there for me during some of the worst times of my life is one person for whom I would do almost anything—except be a therapist. Psychotherapy is one of the few services in which professional reciprocity is rarely appropriate. There is probably no other healing work in which one must be both so close and yet so distant. I know he understands, but the inequity of the situation bothers us both. We want to talk more, but he has a roomful of expectant women, so we kiss good-bye and make our usual overextended promises to stay in touch.

April 14, 1990

We throw a surprise fortieth anniversary party for my parents. It's an ambitious undertaking. We've invited all the Boston relatives and the New York friends. We gather at the hotel party room several hours before the event. The force of the six Manning siblings coming together is like a gale wind that gathers speed as it moves up the coast. We pick up intensity as we go along, till we leave the "outlaws" behind, each of them warning that we'd better calm down. They become outsiders at that point, commiserating with one another about what it's like to be married to such hyper people.

Storms threaten to explode at any moment. I lay out the napkins. Sarah sweeps by and automatically redoes them. Rachel criticizes both of us and does them her way. Priscilla insists that we have misjudged the amount of alcohol we'll need. She and Chip get into it, running down the guest list and ticking off who drinks what versus how much we have. Chip clearly resents his judgment being questioned. Mark refuses to go to the liquor store one more time, citing his tentative hold on sobriety. There are the usual outbursts, the contrite apologies, and the whispered asides to momentary allies about how uptight everyone else is.

Twenty years has changed our looks, but it hasn't budged the dynamics of our interactions. As children, we ate dinner before my parents. After serving dinner, my mother retreated to the living room with a book and a drink. By that time of day, the fragile peace with which the six of us inhabited the same space was at its most tenuous. Dinner ground rules were clear. You had to eat all your dinner or no dessert. You could not get up from the table until everyone was finished. You could not hit, push, or kick. You could not throw food.

These rules were adhered to religiously in my mother's presence and blatantly disregarded the second she opened her book. This was the time to get in your licks. Dinner was a full-contact sport. What started out as innocently swinging your legs under a table where ten other legs dangled slowly became combative. The arc increased as your leg moved out in space and then oh-so-accidentally brushed the leg of the enemy of the moment. All the action was "under the table." No eyewitnesses to tattle. These moves became so finessed over time that one could deliver a kick that actually seemed to come from another side of the table.

Food was illegally discarded to the always appreciative and nondiscriminating dog or through the slots in the radiator. If you were really daring, you could make a quick trip to the garbage can or perform the ultimate heroic act of flushing the food down the toilet. It wasn't just the act of throwing away food that was so significant. It was the precondition that discarding disgusting food required truces between warring factions. All you needed after a perfectly executed rim shot into the garbage can was the revenge of a sister who was convinced that it was you who kicked her under the table. She would yell in her most righteous, whiny, superior ("You may be older than me, but I've got you by the short hairs now") voice, "Mom, Martha is wasting food," a capital offense in our household. These betrayals had to be avoided at all costs.

The best way of accomplishing this was to get everyone involved in the act. In colluding to commit waste together, you knew you would be safe from discovery. The brother you had nailed with a bread ball just two minutes earlier would momentarily abandon his grievance so he could unload his awful meat loaf. The sister who had just told you she hated your "ugly guts" would ally with you for the collective goal of purging the table of all remaining lima beans. This had to be accomplished in the limbo between quiet and chaos. Silence in our house was always cause for suspicion. But we were artists in this domain, with the "big kids" imparting their wisdom to the "little kids" with the solemnity of a religious ceremony.

April 18, 1990

Everything about me seems slightly off. My sleep, which is usually rock solid, is disturbed. Every morning I wake up a bit earlier. On a day-to-day basis it doesn't seem like much. But the cumulative effect is that over the past few months, I'm sleeping about two hours less than my usual. It's alright in the mornings when I can use the time to get more work done. However, I hit the wall in the afternoons, when the days begin to feel just too damn long. It's like I'm watching a Technicolor movie that is slowly fading to black and white.

April 25, 1990

Wednesday is my unscheduled day. No patients. No classes. I use the time for paperwork, preparation, and errands. But it is noon and I can't seem to get started. I find myself walking around the house like a stranger, overwhelmed at everything on my list of things to do. I am foggy and disconnected. I'm infusing caffeine, but I get nothing from it but trembling fingers.

Brian has two cancellations and comes home early. He is puzzled to see me lying on the couch, something I do only with severe injuries or high fevers. He asks if I feel the way I look—gray. I look down and see that he is right. I am dressed in my bag-lady uniform, drooping old sweatpants with more holes than material, a ragged turtleneck, tousled hair, no makeup, socks, or underwear. He asks if I've gone out "looking like that." I remember my trip to the drugstore and get defiant, "Yeah, so?" He shrugs and I can tell he is glad that he wasn't with me. There's a part of me that loves to go out into the world looking like a total slob. I guess it's my way of saying, "Fuck it, I don't give a shit about what anyone thinks I look like."

And yet, another part of me knows that under the defiance, the way I look is a reflection of the way I feel, a walking advertisement of myself as a loser.

May 8, 1990

Annie has been moved to Hospice. The support nursing care for her at home isn't enough anymore. She is in too much pain, and the seizures are more violent and frequent. I drive to the hospice in a car that complains every inch of the trip, sputtering and coughing and threatening to give out on me any minute. Hospice is in a lovely residential neighborhood near the hospital. It is early evening by the time I get there. Spring seems finally to be here. People are working in their gardens, and the air is rich with smells of freshly turned earth and flowers.

I brace myself for the transition to the typical hospital sights and smells of sickness. But the place is much more like home than hospital. Annie's room is large, with rugs and easy chairs, print curtains on the windows, and flowers everywhere. I meet her sister and brother-in-law, who make small talk for several minutes and then leave me alone with her. Annie is in bed, resting against several pillows. I can tell immediately that she is in pain, despite the morphine I know she's getting. She struggles for a smile when she sees me, fighting to keep her eyes open. Her lips are cracked and dry, making it hard for her to talk. She lifts her head a bit and motions for the water. I pour a few ounces out of a plastic pitcher and hold the glass with a straw to her lips, supporting her neck as she drinks. She leans back against the pillows and says, "You came." I chuckle and tell her that with the three messages she had people leave for me today, it seemed like a command performance. She laughs, but it looks like even that makes her tired and she sinks farther into her pillows, and tells me, "I needed you to come tonight." With the slow motion of effort and agony, she raises her hand and covers her eyes. I ask how bad the pain is and she tells me that the morphine helps, but not enough. The amount of morphine it would take to knock out her pain would probably depress her respiration and hasten her death.

I feel uncomfortable in this room that is meant to be so comfortable. I don't know what I'm supposed to do. But it's Annie who's calling the shots now, so I follow her lead. She extends her hand on the bed and inches it over to the bed rail where mine is resting. I take her hand and it seems to ease her a bit. For the next hour she slips in and out of sleep, sometimes in mid-sentence. We talk about the flowers in her garden right now, her daughter, and our work together.

She wants me to know the best thing I ever said to her. I scan my memory for some great piece of wisdom I might have shared with her, but nothing comes to mind.

She turns to me and says, "Remember when I called to tell you the cancer came back? Remember what you said?"

I try hard to remember, but I can't.

She continues, "You got really choked up and then you said, 'This really sucks.'"

I wait for her to articulate whatever brilliant insight I had shared. Then I realize that was it. All of it. Years of training and experience in psychotherapy and "This really sucks" had the most impact in months of work with this dying woman? I feel foolish and inept.

She opens her eyes, stares at me through tears, and whispers, "And it really does, you know, it really sucks."

All I can do is swallow hard, and stop fighting so hard not to cry. I shake my head and agree, "It really does."

She closes her eyes again and grimaces in pain, crying, "Martha, it hurts so bad." I stroke her arm and hand and shush her like I would soothe a young child. She settles a bit and says groggily, "Don't leave just yet." I promise I will sit with her for a while, but encourage her to try to sleep. I bring my head close to her ear and whisper to her our fight song, "How Can I Keep from Singing?" As she settles into sleep, now the last lines seem most fitting. In my shaky, off-key voice I sing them to her, not strong and triumphant anymore, but sweet and slow like a lullaby.

> Through all the tumult and the strife, I hear that music
>   ringing;
> It sounds and echoes in my soul;
> How can I keep from singing?
>
> What though the tempest 'round me roar, I hear the truth it
>   liveth.
> What though the darkness 'round me close, songs in the
>   night it giveth.
> No storm can shake my inmost calm, while to that rock I'm
>   clinging.
> Since love is lord of heaven and earth,
> How can I keep from singing?

She sleeps, free for a while from the fear and the pain. I continue to sit there, more for myself than for her. After a few minutes, I notice that the evening sun has faded and the room is dark. I bend over and kiss her forehead. Knowing that we have reached the limits of medicine and psychotherapy, I call upon the only one left that I can think of. In words that are more a command than a prayer, I whisper, "God bless her."

May 11, 1990

I dread Fridays. Sima, the cleaning lady, comes and I wake up prepared for my weekly dose of shame. Her time at our house is getting shorter and shorter, and even by my slipshod standards, she gives the house the most cursory of cleanings. In my worst feelings, I recognize that "cursory" is sometimes the only appropriate treatment plan for a "terminal case." Maybe our household is just a domestic terminal case. I never felt this humiliation from my mother, and she ran a pretty tight ship. My grandmother, on the other hand, was known to leave notes on her children's beds that said things like, "I cried when I saw this room."

This morning Sima lectures me on being firmer with Keara about her room, which admittedly is a pigsty. I tell Sima that I don't expect her to clean it and that she can just close the door. She begins to tell me about her son's new girlfriend, who is not good enough for him. I look harried and she stops, saying, "Oh, go ahead. You're in a hurry. You still need to do your hair and put on your makeup."

I'm puzzled and stop to correct her, "But I already have." I stick my face out a little so she can look closer and appreciate my efforts.

She surveys me for a second and just says, "Oh."

In only a few minutes this woman has let me know that both my house and I look like shit. I can't believe I'm paying for this. The bottom line is that the house still looks better than when I do it myself. She will probably have to steal the silver or torch the house before I fire her.

May 12, 1990

We are at a party at John and Jennifer's. Lately I find myself more and more resistant to going out socially. What always sounds like a good idea at the time of the invitation feels like an imposition when it actually comes time to get dressed, put on makeup, and be nice to people. My idea of a dream Saturday night these days is eating take-out Chinese food on the couch with Brian and watching videos in our bathrobes.

It is good to see John and Jen, but I feel stiff and awkward with most of the people there, who are strangers. I am losing my touch at making conversation and find myself hanging in corners, happier to observe than participate. Jennifer introduces me to other therapists. Just what I want to do, talk about work, which of course is all there is to talk about, since we usually have absolutely nothing else in common. We exchange the usual pleasantries about office locations and types of patients. I gulp my wine in several swallows, which allows me to hold up my empty glass and excuse myself.

Brian is in the dining room with two guys who look like they aren't talking about anything serious. I insinuate myself into their group and discover to my relief that I am on home turf. It's the Catholic School Conversation. Attendance at Catholic school before 1965 confers lifetime membership in an exclusive club, like the Fraternal Order of Police. Despite differences in age, sex, financial status, or location, the experience of having had your knuckles rapped by ruler-toting women in black-and-white robes is a unifying force. No matter where you are, this membership can be whipped out in social emergencies when the conversation breaks down. We compare our school experiences with those of our children, who, not surprisingly, attend "public school." Brian recalls how we learned to utter the words *public school* with a combination of such contempt and pity for the poor heathen children who attended them. We laugh about the perversity of so much of what we learned: lurid descriptions and pictures of martyrs being boiled in oil, saints having their tongues cut out, graphic, sleep-robbing descriptions of the leper colonies of Father Damien, even a recorded rendition of St. Maria Goretti, patroness of teenage girls, complete with the heavy breathing of the man who attacks her, yelling, "Submit or die." And Maria, pinned beneath him, declaiming, "Death, but not sin," which is precisely what she gets. One of the guys recalls that the worst for him was a brown volume on the bookshelf in his living room called *A Doctor at Calvary*. It was an excruciatingly detailed book about the physiological parameters of Christ's crucifixion, setting the record straight on such gruesome details as the actual placement of the nails—not in the hands and feet, but the wrists and ankles, better for holding. Christ's entire crucifixion, the spiritual bedrock of our religion, is reduced to explicit and ridiculous medical trivia. In the security of adulthood, we can laugh about that craziness without the combination of rapt fascination and horror that we experienced as impressionable Catholic children.

We continue to trade stories until Pam, our baby-sitter, calls with an emergency message for me. I am to call someone named Jim at a phone number I don't immediately recognize. It is noisy in the kitchen, the place where people always seem to congregate at a party. I scrunch into a corner and stick a finger in one ear to lower the noise. I dial the number, get the muffled voice of a woman, and ask for Jim. I put on my most professional voice and say, "This is Dr. Manning. I'm returning your call."

He says, "Martha, you may not remember me. We met last week at Hospice." I feel my hand tighten around the phone. "I am Annie's brother-in-law." I wait to hear what I already know. "Annie died twenty minutes ago."

"I am so sorry," I tell him. "Was anyone with her?"

"We were all here. I know it sounds trite, but it was so peaceful. Bob asked me to let you know that Annie will be in her room for a while. Father Steve is on his way over and there will be some sort of informal service. He asked me to invite you."

I thank him and hang up. John and Jennifer's house is no more than five minutes away from Hospice. I whisper my good-byes to Jennifer. Brian assures me he can catch a ride home. I drive to Hospice. I have met most of Annie's family in the past few months. They clear a path to Annie's bed. She is wearing a peach silk bed jacket with a paisley scarf around her head. Total stillness now replaces the tension of her pain. I touch her hand, still warm, and stroke her cheek.

Her husband puts a hand on my back and says, "You meant so much to her."

"And she to me," I tell him.

Father Steve arrives with a little briefcase that almost looks like a doctor's satchel. He invites us to gather around Annie's bed. He has brought several copies of *The Book of Common Prayer.*

Annie was a convert to the Episcopal church, so most of her family are as much in the dark as I am about what comes next. We bunch up close together to share the prayer books. He is gracious in helping us follow along and telling us when to answer him in the litany of prayers. "Depart, O Christian soul, out of this world," he reads. "May your rest be this day in peace, and your dwelling place in the Paradise of God."

Together, we read the last prayer: "Keep watch, dear Lord, with those who work or watch or weep this night, and give your angels charge over those who sleep. Tend the sick, Lord Christ; give rest to the weary, bless the dying, soothe the suffering, pity the afflicted, shield the joyous, and all for your love's sake. Amen."

The simplicity of the prayer, its inclusivity, and the unfamiliar words recited in unison by the people she loved must be giving Annie such pleasure right now.

We take our turns approaching her one more time. I kiss her forehead and in that moment I remember us together in my office several months ago. Pete Seeger is belting out "How Can I Keep From Singing?" on the boom box and Annie has her eyes closed in rapt meditation, breathing in the enthusiasm, the tenacity, the transcendence of the music. Her body tells a tale of fragility. But her spirit doesn't buy it. When the last strains of the song fade, she opens her eyes, sits up, and pounds her fist into the arm of the chair in a gesture of victory. Then she looks at me, beaming, and proclaims with the conviction of a preacher at a revival meeting, "Yesss!"

June 8, 1990

Keara is twelve today and is marking the occasion with the ritual slumber party. Having spent years as a central figure in Keara's birthdays, I now find myself peripheral. I am necessary for the shopping, invitations, cooking, cleaning, and decorating, but the actual party doesn't need me anymore. I have become invisible.

Girls fall through the door, arms laden with gifts and sleeping bags, shrieking as they see one another. I pay the pizza delivery man, and they are grabbing from the boxes before I can place them on the table. They swarm around the food and inhale it, jabbering while they eat. I find myself mentally practicing the Heimlich maneuver.

They comb their hair constantly and scrutinize one another's clothes. They look at themselves in anything that offers a reflection. One girl admires herself in my toaster.

Over time, both pitch and volume increase. They tell their stories simultaneously, reminding me of their play years ago. They punctuate these stories with such urgent expressions—*"Oh no!"* and *"Oh my God!"*—that I jump up and run down to see who is in danger. They become silent and awkward when I invade their territory. Assuring me that nothing is wrong, they patiently watch me climb the stairs like burglars waiting for people to leave the house.

They are all breast buds and braces. Big feet and long skinny legs, with faces that have yet to wrestle the torments of acne. They exude the innocence and vitality of early adolescence, yet to be tempered by the confusion and the storms to come.

Who are these girls in my living room? They are like strangers to me now. I don't know how much is due to my feeling lousy and how much is just plain getting old. These are the same children who in pastel party dresses held my hands and sang ring-around-the-rosy. I see the girl who cried bitterly when she learned the difficult rule that the present you bring to the party doesn't go home with you. I see the girl who for years has claimed the same rose in the same corner of the cake.

I see the homesick girl I held well into the night of the first slumber party, long after my own child was asleep. These are the same girls, and I am the same mother. But so much has changed. Now I am "the lady upstairs," a barely tolerated intruder. I envy their raucous energy and wish it were contagious.

Three hours into the party, Keara, the classic only child, comes upstairs, as she has at every slumber party, to tell me that it has all been a big mistake. Overwhelmed by the invasion of her territory, she wants to call the whole thing off. I quote the great modern philosopher Lesley Gore and tell her, "It's your party, you can cry if you want to." I recognize that she has once again hit the inevitable wall, when she realizes that the reality of this party will never live up to the weeks of fantasy about it. She finally pulls herself together after my hugs, kisses, and general maternal ministrations and runs back downstairs into the fray. I am relieved because it proves I have a resilient child. But I'm even more relieved because I have no intention of driving nine girls home so late at night.

That crisis over, I settle down with my book, knowing full well that before the night is over someone will want to go home, someone will hurt someone else's feelings, and someone will run a fever, throw up, or both. This year it doesn't much matter. My sleep has been so awful over these past months, I'll actually be glad for the company.

They finally settle down to sleep at 4:00 A.M. I creep downstairs to survey the damage. The potato chips have withered in the bowl. The M & M's have melted, the onion dip has crusted over. The remains of a foam pillow are scattered around the room. When I reach into the refrigerator for ice, I find the smallest bra I've ever seen stashed in the freezer.

Arrayed around the living room are ten sleeping girls. Their sweet faces at rest remind me that, even in my own sleeplessness, one of the great joys of parenthood is admiring the beauty of sleeping children. These girls are straddling childhood and adolescence plugged into Walkmans, but hugging their teddy bears or special blankets, surreptitiously brought along and pulled out for safety in the dark. They have made a valiant stand against the night, defying good sense and fatigue, and have surrendered finally to sleep. As lousy as I feel, it is a comfort to know that the pleasures of children can still penetrate my darkness. This chance to watch them sleep, these ring-around-the-rosy girls, full of promise and possibility, gives me hope for the future, however fleeting.

June 11, 1990

I'm into the homestretch. Teresa is my last patient. Her head is obscuring the clock on the shelf above her chair. If only she'd shift a bit, I could catch the time. Instead, I am reduced to the furtive looks at the wristwatch that therapists cultivate, along with skills like suppressing giggles, yawns, and expressions of outright horror. It's 3:42. Eight minutes left.

The session drags on. We get nowhere. Teresa is married to her unhappiness and shows no signs of initiating a separation. Two minutes left. Time to wrap it up. I want to be on the road by 4:00. The answering machine clicks on. Damn. I realize that I haven't yet changed the message to say I'll be away for the rest of the week. Now I'll have to call the person back.

I am going on retreat. There is a Trappist monastery about ninety minutes away, and I'm all signed up. Consistent with the Trappist way of life, it is a silent retreat. No talking. Four days of no talking. Maybe this is what I need. A total break in the action, a time-out, a chance to slow down and take stock of the way my life seems to be careening out of control.

Teresa leaves, sighing. I press the Play button on the machine, hoping like hell that it isn't anything important. It's just some guy trying to interest me in disability insurance. Forget it.

I'm out of here.

The drive is a fitting introduction to the retreat, with a growing sense of distance from my everyday existence. The first hour is frustrating late-afternoon traffic, with lights that keep coming and seem always to be red. The streets are congested and cluttered with row after row of stores and fast-food places. But then the road opens up, and all I see are creeks, farms, and long stretches of mountains. The other cars disappear and I am alone. My blasting, raunchy music becomes loud and intrusive. I turn the radio off and let myself enjoy the silent approach of evening over the mountains.

I arrive when the sun is low in the sky, making everything golden. The mountains are purple, like the heather hills in Ireland. Brother Francis introduces himself as the guest master. He calls me "Marie Manning," blushes, and apologizes. The psychologist in me is curious about the story behind that one, but I let it go.

He tells me that I am welcome at the services that punctuate the monks' days. The first one begins at 3:30 A.M., which I decide ranks right up there with hair shirts and self-flagellation. The retreat is totally unstructured. The only things he requests are silence and prompt attendance at meals.

I unpack and walk up the hill to the abbey chapel to attend the vesper service. The chapel is plain and dark. The monks enter silently with the ringing of a bell. Two monks lead the chanting. It is the feast of Elizabeth Seton—as they describe her, "wife, mother, teacher, and foundress." There are probably few other saints with whom I have as many things in common.

The chanting is hypnotic. Sitting in the sanctuary of the back row, in the warm and the dark, with the wind rising outside, I close my eyes and let their voices envelop me. I feel my teeth less scrunched together, my jaw less tight, and my breathing deeper. Not bad for two hours.

I don't know what this time holds for me. Part of me wants to set up a schedule, draw up an agenda of things to think about, decisions to make, work to do. I guess this mindset somehow misses the point of a retreat. Maybe it's not just the external noise I'm supposed to be escaping. I could probably stand to give the inner noise a rest as well.

Dinner is right out of one of my favorite lines from Ludwig Bemelmans's children's book *Madeline.*

In two straight lines they broke their bread
brushed their teeth and went to bed.

That's what we look like tonight at dinner. Six women, three by three facing one another. We stand silently and awkwardly as Brother Francis talks about the retreat. He is a quiet, gentle man who is quite earnest about the importance of rest.

I keep waiting for there to be more at dinner. But soup is not just the first course, it is the only course. I wish I'd availed myself of a Big Mac and fries on the way. Luckily, the soup tastes good. I make the profound observation that for a farm, they serve incredibly processed-looking American cheese. Also, they serve Safeway jams, rather than their own Monastery label, which they sell in the gift shop.

Not talking while eating is more self-conscious-making than I expected. It's hard not to be aware of what everyone else is doing. I look right away for the people I think I'd like, or try to figure out who is a nun. Really spiritual stuff like that. There is a big jar of chocolate-chip cookies on the table and I am aware, once again, of my abiding attachment to food. If I could feel one-tenth of that attachment to God, I would probably be in much better shape than I am right now. In a lot of ways.

I feel mixed about being here. On the one hand, I feel myself settling right in, being quiet, having a hunger in me filled. But I also think, "What am I doing here? What about Keara? What about my patients?" I obsess about the responsibilities I am neglecting by being here. In chapel I think about how my anxiety often comes from the wish to be totally in control—even of things I can't possibly control. Who do I think I am? God? Well, on some level, I must. I remember those wonderful lines from *Gitanjali* by the poet Rabindranath Tagore:

Oh fool, to try to carry thyself upon thy own shoulders
Oh beggar, to come and beg at thy own door . . .

It is 7:30 P.M. Time for compline, the last service of the day, and the monks come together and offer their prayers to the night. Through the service the room grows darker, with a final light shining on a simple statue of Mary. They chant, "Do not fear the terrors of the night or the arrow that flies by day." At the end of the service each monk is blessed by the abbot and slowly leaves the chapel. Then the abbot comes to the back of the chapel and blesses the retreatants. My first impulse is to kiss him good-night, which I'm instantly glad I resist doing.

Compline brings back such strong memories of childhood. Of coming into the living room with all five brothers and sisters and kissing our parents good-night. No matter what messes or conflicts or trouble we had managed to get into, the kisses always came—constant, accepting, forgiving. I can still smell those times, everyone coming down bathed with shining hair and brushed teeth, all of us with different degrees of reluctance about giving ourselves up to the night.

It reminds me of the importance of ritual in our lives. We lose tolerance for the rituals that children develop to protect themselves from the fear of going to sleep. To close the day, to ease into the night, to tolerate the shadows of the dark, to ask "Will I come back? Will you come back?" we need some help. We need those extra drinks of water, that certain story said in the exact same way. The back has to be rubbed, and the blankets smoothed, just so. And the song, the song must be sung over and over. With Keara it was always James Taylor. Now she refuses to believe that fact and claims nausea each time one of his songs comes on the radio. But I remember.

She doesn't need the rituals any longer. In fact, over the past year she has specifically told me, "You don't need to tuck me in anymore." But I have to admit that I still hold on to one part of the ritual. There is never a night when I don't go into her room for what we call the "after-sleep kiss." I kiss her cheek and smooth her sweaty hair. I look at her teddy bear tucked under her arm and an open book still in her hands. I stand in the midst of a room that is always too messy and I see things that I will chastise her about in the morning. Even in those first years of her life, when I had abandoned all experience of religion, my only prayer was for her: "Good-night, sweet child. Please God, protect her in the darkness and bless her in the light."

I plan to sleep through the 3:30 A.M. vigil. I don't need to prove that I can get up that early. Hell, I spend half my life doing that, just trying to get a jump on the day.

I settle under the covers in my solid narrow bed. Through the windows I can see the mountains in the moonlight. It is magic.

> So good-night, little girls,
> Thank the lord you are well
> And now go to sleep, said Miss Clavell
> And she turned out the lights,
> and she closed the door
> And that's all there is
> There isn't any more.

Retreat Day Two

I've been reading the psalms—at first silently, then in whispers. I understand them better when I speak them. There is one I love—Psalm 38:

> O Lord, all my desire is before you;
> From you my groaning is not hid.
> My heart throbs; my strength forsakes me;
> The very light of my eyes has failed me.
> My friends and neighbors stand back
> Because of my affliction;
> My neighbors stand afar off.

It's incredible to me that we never learned the psalms as children. All that time and energy memorizing the catechism when the real thing was right here. It's like memorizing *TV Guide* rather than watching the show.

I sit in the sun and the silence and read the prayers. I begin to cry. As I slow down, the frantic activity and noise of my life is replaced by a quiet ache, an emptiness I can't quite name. I suspect it's been following me for a while. I've just been able to outrun it.

The toilets overflow on the first floor. I hear this huge gurgling noise and then a WHOOSH, and suddenly there is sewage all over the bathroom floor. I open my door and look down the hall to see if this is a personal misfortune or a more universal phenomenon. As I stick my head out the door, the woman across the hall from me looks out also. I've noticed her at meals. She's in her late twenties and looks like she hasn't received word yet that the 1960s are over. She wears a long Indian-print skirt and Birkenstocks, and could braid the hair under her arms if she chose to. She breaks the silence.

"Is there shit all over your floor?" she asks.

I make a face and answer, "Yeah." We stand there for a moment, recovering the silence.

Then she nods her head several times and says, "Cosmic."

I shake my head and reply, "Metaphor."

Retreat Day Three

The harsh realities of life creep in, even here. On my way out for a walk, I notice that my car has a flat tire. I get really angry. "This is just great. This is all I need. Even on retreat I can't get away from the hassles." I act like this one thing has the power to obliterate the goodness of this experience. It's like diffusing a bit of black paint into a totally white space. Pretty soon, even if it was only a small amount, it turns the whole thing to gray. But I'm not dealing with paint here, I'm dealing with my life. With experiences that aren't additive. A bad thing happening does not reverse a good thing. My life is not just one big equation in which I add, subtract, and balance to figure out how happy I deserve to be. But that's exactly how I live.

I get up the nerve to tell Brother Francis that I have a flat and ask if one of the monks might be able to check it out. He listens carefully and thoughtfully, and answers, "We'll see." I stand there stuck. "We'll see"? What kind of answer is that? Is he saying yes or no? I get really nervous because I see that he thinks our conversation is finished. What do I do now? Do I press the point? I need to get organized. I need details. What does he really mean? When I say "We'll see" to Keara, it's usually the coward's way of saying no. I'm not quite ready to take the full burst of her displeasure at being denied what she wants, so I string her along, hoping that time will make her forget. Is that what he's doing with me? What if it really means no? What if I'm stuck here? Forever? This is a nice place, but I don't think I can go too much longer without a Diet Coke, a roll in the sheets, or a racquetball game.

I continue to catastrophize about my predicament until I realize that I have to back off. I have to trust that he heard my request, that he understands how important it is. I decide that I have no alternative but to wait it out, trying to have faith that this man will help me. As anxious as the whole thing makes me, I see that this is exactly the struggle for me in trusting in God. Not only do I ask God to do things, I am usually very careful to specify exactly how these things should be accomplished. And I am fairly intolerant of any deviations from my plan.

batical, but told me when we ended that if I needed to check in with him, I could.

I think back to my three years of work with him. I went in originally because I felt anxious and panicky a lot of the time, a condition I had experienced throughout my life on a smaller scale. But with the demands of a young child, an academic career, and a psychotherapy practice, I found myself in deeper water and thought I could use some swimming lessons.

A friend recommended him. Being a therapist myself, I found consulting a therapist a bit strange at first. But I comforted myself that most therapists have their own psychotherapy at some point in their professional lives and rationalized that this was not some personal failing on my part, but rather a quest for personal growth. It was bullshit, but I find a self-deception quite comforting.

I don't know what I was expecting four years ago, on my first visit, but it wasn't what I got. There was nothing so extraordinary about him—on the outside, anyway. No outward signs of his power to heal. He was coming apart "clotheswise," which I figured was a good sign, since I was coming apart "selfwise." He was missing a button on a shirt that didn't match his pants or his tie. He wore wild-and-crazy socks with a pair of dull honest shoes. But I didn't think of those things as important. Not much anyway. He had a turquoise and onyx cufflink on one wrist, and a black metal binder clip on the other. And I thought to myself, "This guy must know what it's like to come apart a little—the ups on the one hand, the downs on the other." He told me that I might want to interview other therapists, which had been my plan. But, for some reason, the outrageous socks and the ersatz cufflink settled it. I knew he was the one.

I told him I was anxious. He said that's not all I was. He said I'd had a low-level depression most of my life and he recommended antidepressant medicine in addition to

*psychotherapy. I was shocked at the suggestion and protested,
"But I've felt like this all my life and I've gotten along okay."*

*"All that means," he answered, "is that you have a high
tolerance for pain and a lot of determination."*

*My training as a clinical psychologist had historically
rejected the biological approaches to panic and depression. But he
reinterpreted the story of my life and the history of my family and
challenged my preconceptions about the total ascendancy of
insight over pills. Because my grandmother responded well to
imipramine, he decided to start with that. I reluctantly tried the
pills. Several weeks into taking the medicine I realized that I
actually felt good. Not up, not down, just good. It was as if a
switch had been turned on. I treaded lightly that whole day,
afraid that it might evaporate with a sudden move, a nap, or a
sneeze. But it lasted. I became a believer.*

*While the medicine put me on a more even keel than I'd
been in my life, the psychotherapy turned me upside down and
inside out. It made me look at my life from every perspective
except the constricted rigid vertical one I was used to. He led me
down a hall of mirrors and invited me to try on all the images,
even the ones that seemed weird or wild. He helped me mourn my
miscarriages. He challenged my notion that the long line of gifted,
creative women in my family came to a dead stop at my birth,
inviting the artist-in-hiding to join the scientist-in-residence. He
laughed at the clown in me, and laughed harder at the judge,
always stern and mean to myself. He shrugged with indifference
to questions he couldn't answer, which made me nervous. "If
you're such a great medicine man, you should know," I would say.
But he insisted that I was wrong. I realized that if he didn't have
all the answers, then maybe I didn't have to have them either.
Maybe shrugging your shoulders is a tool of the trade. Not a hole
in your pocket or knowledge or power, but a way to say to people,*

"No one has all the answers, honey, and you can look to me or some other joker, but they still aren't there. It's tough. But it's true." I considered myself "cured." But I guess there are no lifetime warranties on cures.

Fifteen minutes after I leave a message on his machine, Jeremy calls back. I tell him that I think I am slipping. He says he can hear it in my voice. He recommends Kay Jamison for psychotherapy and encourages me to give the medicines another look. I call around and get the name of Lew Bigelow, a local psychopharmacologist. The thought of switching to other people is painful, but I have no choice. Something is wrong and I will not allow it to get out of control.

June 18, 1990

Dr. Lew Bigelow's office is not easy to find. The clusters of two-story brick buildings all look the same and the numbers are hard to read. I spot his name on a second-floor window and climb the stairs with the trepidation I experience whenever I meet someone new. His waiting room consists of a small antique bed converted into a couch sitting in a hallway. Piles of very old *New Yorker* and *Harvard* magazines compete for space with the typical white-noise machine used to protect patients from thin walls and noise that carries. Waiting to meet him, I realize how anxious I am and how much I don't want to do this. Every week I blithely ask new patients the seemingly innocuous questions, "What brings you here?" and "How can I help you?" Now, as I anticipate this appointment, I realize how those questions are so much easier to ask than answer. How does one condense a life into an answer?

Fifteen minutes after the appointed time, Dr. Bigelow walks down the hall. He is a long man, for whom the ceiling almost seems too low. Shaking my hand firmly, he says formally, "Dr. Manning, Dr. Bigelow." His office smells like cigarette smoke but seems comfortable enough, with antiques, a worn Oriental rug, and engaging paintings on the walls. He sits behind a small table, which doesn't totally accommodate his legs, in a black-and-gold Cornell chair. I am struck by how uncomfortable it looks, and how different it is from the big leather reclining chair and ottoman in my office.

He poses the standard litany of questions, recording the answers on a thick pile of loose-leaf paper. When he asks me how I feel on my current medicine, I tell him, "Okay, but I'm a little zoned out."

He looks totally perplexed, like I just switched from English to Japanese, and repeats politely, "Zoned out?"

I silently give him ten demerits for having to ask the meaning of a phrase I use so commonly and begin to doubt seriously whether this is going to be a good match. "You know," I explain, "like the 'Twilight Zone.'"

He frowns. I try again, "Like spaced out, in the ozone, out of it."

I hit pay dirt with "out of it" and we are back on the same wavelength, but I feel less and less articulate over the hour. He asks difficult questions: "When did you start having symptom X?" "On a scale of one to ten, rate your . . ." Forty-five minutes into the interview, I mentally cross him off the list.

But in the last five minutes, the question-and-answer volley stops. In the open space of silence, I find myself telling this stranger that I am afraid. That I feel myself falling and I don't know how to stop. He puts down his pen, pushes away his paper, and very quietly says, "I know." For the entire hour he has exactingly scribbled almost everything I've said. But this, the most important piece, he does not record. He doesn't need to. I can tell that he already understands.

June 20, 1990

I am hungover from the continually interrupted sleep I've been having lately. I never sleep more than two hours at a stretch. Each time I wake up, I think it must be time to rise (not shine) for the day. But it's always only 2:00 A.M. or 3:00 A.M. or 4:00 A.M. The nights are getting longer and the sleep is getting shorter. I am down to a total of four hours of sleep a night. Falling asleep is no problem. It's staying asleep that's so hard. I've pulled out old hypnosis tapes. I try the same relaxation inductions I do with my patients. I count backward. Sometimes I even pray. Lew is working his way down the list of medicines that might help (a pinch of a more sedating antidepressant here, a dash of tranquilizer there). All to no avail. This week I tried some heavy-duty sleeping pills that he said would knock out a charging rhino. But they didn't work on me.

There is an excruciating loneliness in waiting out the hours till morning, again and again and again. Time moves more slowly, and the fact that everyone else is at rest makes me feel so separate, so alone. I long to recover what comes so easily to everyone else.

I try to be productive, but it has to be mindless activity since it takes longer and longer each day for my brain to get into gear. I do the laundry. I wash the kitchen floor. I paint my nails. I wait till the first signs of daylight and do the grocery shopping at 5:00 A.M. I'd do it earlier, but our neighborhood isn't particularly safe, and Brian made me promise that I wouldn't start my errands until daybreak.

In the old days of two- and three-day sleepless blitzes on projects and proposals, I countered people's cautions with the wisdom that "No one ever died from lack of sleep." But right now, in the cold silence of 3:35 A.M., I conclude that no one ever really lived from lack of sleep either.

June 21, 1990

Since I've been on the MAO (monoamine oxidase) inhibitors, a different family of drugs than I've taken in the past, it's been harder and harder to pee. Many of the antidepressants have what is called "urinary hesitancy" as a side effect, meaning that you sit there for an eternity before you actually produce anything. Up until now, it's been a nuisance side effect, one I don't like but can basically tolerate. But the hesitancy is turning into outright refusal and I'm getting very uncomfortable. This morning I just couldn't go. My bladder was filled to what I consider capacity, but nothing would come. At first it's like those long car trips where you think you'll start a flood in the car if you don't find a rest stop immediately. But then it gets worse, it's hard to stand up straight. I run the water in the bathroom sink. I take a hot bath. I imagine waterfalls. Nothing. I call Lew, who tells me to see a urologist. I get a referral from a friend, tell the receptionist my problem, and she encourages me to come immediately.

Luckily the doctor's office is close. Before even taking much of a history, he uses a catheter and drains the engine. The relief is incredible. As the procedure wears on and I keep producing, the urologist says, "You must have been really uncomfortable." He sends the nurse twice for another container. When it is all over, I sit up and he holds up the different containers, like I just won some kind of urinary output derby.

I get dressed and meet him in his office with the typical imposing mahogany desk, the stacks of fat books, and every bit of wall space filled with some kind of framed statement attesting to his competence. I tell him about the new medicine and my suspicion that it is related to the current problem. He looks it up in the *Physicians' Desk Reference*, doesn't see acute urinary retention in the list of side effects from the drug, and dismisses my hypothesis. I am always amazed at the way physicians treat the *PDR* like the damned Holy Bible. It's basically a collection of drug summaries composed by the drug companies themselves, who are never going to be the ones shouting bad side effects from the rooftops. I ask him for his diagnosis. He tells me that there is a small chance that it could be multiple sclerosis. But he leans back in his chair and says that it is more likely "hysterical." I can't believe what I've just heard.

"Hysterical?" I repeat.

He nods and says self-righteously, "Maybe you can put your professional training and experience to use in managing it."

My face grows hotter by the second, my already dry mouth gets drier. With that shred of wisdom, I see that he thinks our consultation is over. He schedules a follow-up appointment for the end of the week.

I am speechless. As a therapist, I have heard so many stories from women patients of doctors and rampant sexism, but other than being called "honey" and "sweetie" by some of my early gynecologists, I've been lucky. But now I am labeled a hysterical woman. And the worst thing about it is that I feel more humiliated than angry. It only lasts a few minutes though, because by the time I reach the elevator, I decide that the man is uniquely qualified to be a urologist, since he is such a complete and total prick.

I call Lew to tell him the diagnosis. He calls the guy an idiot, which makes me feel a whole lot better. In our discussion, we decide that this problem is perhaps related to the dosage of the medicine, and that I should skip a dose and then pick up again at a lower dose.

It works like a charm. I cancel my appointment with the urologist. He actually calls back to ask why I've canceled the appointment. I tell him the reason and he replies, "That's really interesting. You should write that up."

I want to reach through the phone and rip his lungs out, but instead I remain overtly polite and say, "Yeah, maybe I will."

The good news is that the lower dose alleviates the side effects. The bad news is that it doesn't do the depression any favors. Old symptoms return. I feel myself slowing down, slipping back to where I was. Lew decides that despite their effectiveness as antidepressants, the MAOs have such serious side effects for me that they must be abandoned. It is back, once again, to the drawing board.

June 22, 1990

I'm getting less good at faking it. People in my family are noticing and asking what's wrong. My friends give me invitations to talk, to cry. I love them for their caring, but I want to run from it. I have lost their language, their facility with words that convey feelings. I am in new territory and feel like a foreigner in theirs.

I feel like I am rowing against the current. And despite every ounce of energy I can muster, I am making no progress.

sight. Keep going, a foot at a time. *It was only the space of eight houses, a forty-five-second dash along the seawall. But wind and currents conspired with their own designs.*

Twenty minutes passed. We came close enough to shore with a shifting wind that I could jump out of the boat and feel my feet touch bottom. I grabbed hold of the bow and I pulled that damn boat, all the while trying to steady myself against the waves and the pain of the small stones pulling back and forth over my feet. I took a couple of hard waves, swallowing and spitting salt water as I pressed on. Ellen jumped out and we hauled the boat onto shore, up across the stones, to the sand where it would be safe. Mark laughed at the fun he'd had and ran up the beach to the seawall steps. Ellen and I lay by the boat, gulping air between tears of fear and relief. As we looked out at the storm on the water, the distance we fought to cover seemed so insignificant. But the pain in my back and arms told a different story.

It began to thunder and lightning, and Ellen went home. I walked up the beach, still shaken by how quickly things can change and you can be up against such danger in the midst of such seeming safety and security.

I walked through the porch and into the house. Brothers, sisters, and assorted cousins were finishing lunch. My mother called, "Where have you been? You almost missed lunch." I wanted to run in crying and spill it all out to her: how the storm came up so fast, how I thought we would drown, how frightened I was for Mark, how I'd never tried so much and moved so little, how I felt so scared, how I hurt, and how I was still trembling. I wanted to say that for the first time in my life I felt my own fragility and was almost lost to the water.

But I looked out the picture window and saw the coast guard cutter with its lights shining through the rain. I looked at the dining room filled with safe, dry children, and somehow,

I just couldn't. Someone repeated the question, "Where have you been?" I sat down, reached for a peanut butter sandwich, and shrugged, "Nowhere . . . just out."

I wish I could tell people this story, but I never have. Some struggles are so solitary that they drown in words.

June 23, 1990

As my own words fade, the long silences are punctuated with lines of songs and pieces of poems. Fragments of the poem "Song in a Year of Catastrophe," by Wendell Berry, echo in my mind.

> Learn the darkness.
> Gather round you all
> the things that you love, name
> their names, prepare
> to lose them. It will be
> as if all you know were turned
> around within your body.

June 24, 1990

We go to Patricia and Patrick's for dinner. Even feeling lousy, I enjoy the sight of our growing-up children around the table and the reassuring company of old friends. Someone mentions our mutual housecleaner, Sima, in the course of the conversation. I chuckle and say, "Oh, Sima, the bane of my existence. I think we must be the worst people she cleans for."

"You are," Suzanne, the nine-year-old, pipes up brightly.

Patricia puts down her fork and exclaims, "What?"

Suzanne cheerfully continues, "Sima said you are really big slobs."

Even with my dearest friends, who know that it's true, and don't seem to care, I'm still embarrassed. I have been betrayed by my cleaning lady. Somehow, I always assumed a similar confidential relationship between cleaner and client as in other relationships where one person cleans up another person's messes, like therapists, doctors, and lawyers. The house is just going to have to go to hell, like the rest of my life. Living with a private mess is one thing. Going public with it is quite another.

June 25, 1990

I fight the late-afternoon traffic in Georgetown for my first appointment with Dr. Kay Jamison. There is a tiny goldfish pond in front of her townhouse and flowers everywhere. I take a deep breath and ring the doorbell, unaccustomed to coming to someone's house for therapy. When she opens the door, I am surprised at how young she looks. She leads me up a long flight of stairs to her study. The color of the carpeting in her study is exactly the same as mine. Looking around the room, with its order and beauty, I see that the similarity ends there. The large room is lined with shelves from floor to ceiling, filled with books. They appear organized by theme, with as many books on poetry and art as psychology, which I take as a good sign.

She motions me to a pair of flowered armchairs in the center of the room. After a careful history and review of my symptoms she tells me that I am "quite depressed." I can tolerate being labeled "depressed." "Quite depressed" sounds more serious and feels "quite" uncomfortable when applied to me. I tell her how humiliated I am that I can't deal with it myself. I confess my hypocrisy, professing that I can help other people when I am such a mess myself. She responds that some of the best therapists are the ones with the most darkness in their lives and that some of the greatest artists have known the terrible torments of depression. She tells me I have a very moralistic view of depression as a personal weakness and a condition under one's control. She counters with her belief that my depression is an illness. Her emphasis on the biological aspects of depression is surprising to me, coming from a fellow psychologist. As she talks, she says at one point, "People who suffer from depression . . . " I don't hear the rest of the sentence. "Suffer from depression." That's right. It is suffering. A person doesn't just *have* depression. She suffers from it. On the basis of that phrase alone, I know that this woman can help me.

June 26, 1990

In the psychological literature, depression is often seen as a defense against sadness. But I'll take sadness any day. There is no contest. Sadness carries identification. You know where it's been and you know where it's headed. Depression carries no papers. It enters your country unannounced and uninvited. Its origins are unknown, but its destination always dead-ends in you.

June 27, 1990

I'm now in my third week of bronchitis. Every day I get sicker, and my sleep gets even worse. Last night I woke up feeling chilled and desperate, thinking, "Oh no. How long will this last? How will I pay tomorrow?" I live with a constant shaking-crying feeling. I don't know how much longer I can take it.

I spend every free moment curled up on the couch in my office, wrapped in my blanket feeling awful. Brian thinks I should stay home. But I keep going because I've learned over the past months that as bad as things seem, they can always get worse. I don't know how much worse things are going to get.

June 28, 1990

My 10:00 patient is a new referral. I'm already overwhelmed with work, but in this business you take what you get because you're not sure when the inevitable slow times will come. The only thing she told me on the phone was that she was referred by her internist because she is still distraught over the breakup of a relationship more than six months ago.

She is an attorney, working her ass off to make partner in her law firm, which, like most firms, abuses the hell out of its associates. Her clothes are businesslike, but elegant. Her makeup, nails, and hair bear witness to exacting attention. But the professional demeanor with which she conducts herself in the first few minutes of the interview does not feel right to me. She is trying too hard. She reports the breakup of the relationship as if she is presenting a case in court—all facts, no feeling. I lean forward in my chair and comment softly, "How painful that must have been for you." The veneer quickly dissolves into tears.

As I determine the extent of her pain, I switch into gear assessing for the common signs that help to distinguish the reaction to a loss from a clinical depression. Clinicians commit the criteria to memory from the bible of diagnosis—the *Diagnostic and Statistical Manual.*

Depressed mood? Yes.

Markedly diminished interest in almost everything? Yes. I begin to realize that I am working on two checklists, the one on the page in front of me about her, and the other on a page in my head, about myself. So far we're both two for two.

Significant weight loss? No for her. Yes for me.

Sleep difficulties? Yes for her. Yes for me.

Psychomotor retardation or agitation? No for her. Yes for me.

Fatigue? Yes for her. Yes for me.

Feelings of worthlessness and guilt? Yes for her. Yes for me.

Problems with concentration? No for her. Yes for me.

Recurrent thoughts of death, suicide? No for her. Yes for me.

She meets five of the nine criteria, qualifying for the diagnosis of "major depressive episode." I try to defer my horror at meeting nine out of nine criteria until the session is over.

I recommend a consultation with a psychopharmacologist to determine whether medication might be useful. In addition, I strongly recommend psychotherapy, pointing out that the loss of her boyfriend appears to have triggered unresolved pain from the childhood trauma of her mother's early death. We set a regular appointment time and discuss dealing with the inevitable and intrusive questions at work about her request for time off. The rapport between us feels solid and workable. But I wonder to myself how someone who is nine for nine on the depression index can possibly help someone who is "only" five for nine.

In the ten minutes between sessions, I pull out my manual and flip to the section on major depression. I want a second opinion. I do this in those quizzes in women's magazines with the little tests that will answer questions like, "Are you keeping your man satisfied in bed?" or "What does your closet say about your personality." I love those stupid quizzes. I fill them out, add up my score, and then quickly turn to the section that gives me my rating. If I don't like the results, I automatically turn back to the test and take it over. I change answers that were only marginally true, or ones that I've rationalized aren't really true at all, trying to get my score into a more acceptable range. I do that now. But as I work my way down the list, there are no marginal answers, not a single area in which I can "massage the data." In fact, when I turn to another section, called "Major Depression: Melancholic Type," I find that I meet all those criteria as well.

I am rattled for the rest of the day. Seeing myself in black and white turns my subjective experience of depression into an objective one. I'm not an outside observer in this office anymore. I'm a card-carrying, dues-paying member of the club.

June 29, 1990

Lew leaves a message on my machine, asking if I'm interested in a referral. I can't believe it, and play the message back once more. Week after week he gets the blow-by-blow about how lousy I feel. I have arrived at a comfort level with him where I mince no words, do no cosmetic surgery on my symptoms to make myself look better off than I really am. It has been a humbling process for me, and I have just assumed that he has "basket case" written somewhere in my chart. But knowing all that, he still refers me a patient.

Our sessions have loosened up considerably since the first few formal "Dr. Manning, Dr. Bigelow" sessions. It helps me remember that often it takes a while for a doctor and patient to develop a common wavelength. Lew is the only person I have ever known who smokes generic-brand cigarettes. He laughs when I notice and tell him that if he's going to risk his life, he should at least go first class. The worn green binder in which he keeps my file is expanding by the week, with countless lab test results, consultation reports, and session notes. He is a careful clinician who shares my distress when an effective medicine has to be terminated because of potentially dangerous side effects. He is sympathetic with the continual frustration of medicines that work for a month or two, but then must be increased until they hit the ceiling of safety and must be discontinued.

In the last minutes of our sessions, we often discuss our work: interesting or baffling cases, things we have read and how we understand them, critiques of the current research. For me these are not just conversations that kill off the remnants of an hour. After I have focused for an eternity each session on all the problems and the pain, these interchanges validate the part of me that is still very much in the world, still thinking and working and living. When this fellow professional who knows every lousy detail about me shifts for a few minutes to treating me like a respected colleague rather than a depressed patient, he forces me to make that shift as well. He challenges me, in those brief interactions, to acknowledge those aspects of myself that continue to function, despite this nightmare. I'm not sure he knows it, but as shaky as I am right now, these small moments have become as important as the capsules I swallow in the nights to get me through the days.

June 30, 1990

I play a perverse game with myself: What wonderful thing could snap me out of this? I have sampled all the possibilities. Millions of dollars? No. The Nobel Prize? No. Another child? No. Peace on earth? No. No good news or good times. Nothing. And all I can think of is the cruelty of it all. And the incapacitating dread that this time I won't come out. This time it will never end.

July 1, 1990

When you're depressed, everyone has an opinion about what you should do. People seem to think that not only are you depressed, you are also stupid. They are generous to the point of suffocation with their advice. I wonder sometimes, if I had any other illness, whether people would be so free with their admonitions. Probably not. They would concede that what they know is vastly outweighed by what they don't know and keep their mouths shut. People hear the word *depression* and figure that since they've felt down or blue at some point in their lives, they are experts, which is like assuming that because you've had a chest cold, you are now qualified to treat lung cancer.

I keep a running list of advice in my head. I sort it into categories. The first involves those behaviors that shrinks nauseatingly call "nurturance." They include such things as going away for the weekend, buying myself expensive jewelry, getting a manicure, pedicure, haircut, facial, or massage. The next category addresses my various vices: quit Diet Coke, avoid junk food, take vitamins, get more sleep, get more exercise/get less exercise. In the self-improvement domain I am told to throw myself into my work/cut down on my work, see my therapist more frequently/quit my therapist/see the advice-giver's therapist. I am advised to take more medicine/less medicine/different medicine/no medicine. I am told to pray, to meditate, to "journal," to think of people worse off than I ("You think you've got it bad?" therapy). I have been handed the cards of spiritual advisers, chiropractors, bioenergists, herbalists, and a woman who works with crystals.

In the old days, I could shake it all off and gently refuse it. But the humiliation I feel now about being so publicly vulnerable makes me just stand there and absorb it. All their "helpful" comments imply that if I'd only do _____, my problems would be solved. Like it's all within my grasp, able to be managed and mastered, if only I would try harder, longer, better. As I nod my head in polite and pathetic appreciation for their input, I scream inside, "Shut up. Shut up. Unless you've been lost in this particular section of hell yourself, don't you dare try to give me directions."

July 2, 1990

Brian and I have a racquetball court reserved for 9:00. These mornings are so hard. The dread of the day, even a low-key, low-demand day, is overwhelming. I try to shake it off with activity, but my usual morning vigor has evaporated and it takes hours to dispel the clouds inside my head. I don't want to play, but I keep hoping to get a hit of endorphins from the exercise. Automatically I step on the scale in the locker room. I can't believe the reading, step off, and try again. I've lost thirteen pounds in the past four weeks. I know my usual monster appetite has been tamer lately, but I'm still surprised by such a significant loss, especially without trying. From my moldy gym bag, I pull out the unwashed shirt and shorts I wore for the last game. They are wrinkled and smelly and I don't care.

I am clumsy on the court, like I'm wearing someone else's body. My timing is off and I miss the easiest of shots. This once-simple pleasure exceeds my grasp. Brian offers continual encouragement as I attempt to make contact with the ball. I know he is trying to be helpful, but his solicitude annoys the hell out of me. As I bend down to serve, he suggests, "Maybe it would help if you varied your serves a little."

His comment blinds me with anger. "When I want your fucking advice, I'll ask for it," I retort.

His face changes quickly from surprise, to hurt, to outright anger. "Bitch," he mutters, and stomps off the court.

Now it is my turn to be surprised. I wait several minutes and determine that he has no intention of returning.

We retreat to our respective locker rooms and meet in silence at the car. The drive home is eternal. He adopts an air of righteous indignation at being undeservingly blindsided. I am broiling but can't understand why. I attempt to cut the silence with my usual conversation starter in fights, "What's your problem?"

"I am sick of having to tiptoe around you all the time. I am trying to help you and all I get is your anger. I don't deserve it," he tells me.

I know he's right, but I still feel so angry at him. I start to cry, out of a combination of frustration and guilt. I realize that I am sick of his help, of continually feeling like a patient with my own husband. I tell him, "I don't want you to help me. I want you to be with me."

He looks at me like he has no comprehension of the difference between those two things.

"I don't need a therapist-in-residence," I say. "I need a husband."

"I'm not trying to be your therapist," he replies. "What do you want from me?"

"When I tell you how lousy I feel, I don't want to run down my medications with you, I don't want to have to answer your questions, to try to put it all into words. I don't want to listen to a pep talk, or a list of suggestions."

"Then what the hell do you want?" he demands.

"Just hold me. Sit with me. Put your arm around me. Listen as I struggle to tell you what it feels like, without thinking you have to tie it all up in some cohesive clinical bundle. I don't expect you to make this better. I know you can't. But I think you feel that if you just try hard enough, that you can." We drive a few blocks in silence.

He says, "Y'know, Marth, this is hard on me too. . . . I see you slipping and I am scared. . . . I'm losing you, and nothing I try brings you back."

In our first agreement of the morning, I admit, "I know."

We say nothing the rest of the way home. Lugging our gym bags into the house, we greet a sleepy-eyed Keara who has just gotten up. "Good game?" she asks brightly. The look on our faces belies the answer Brian gives her, "Yeah, love, it was just great."

July 6, 1990

We spend a long weekend with my family at the beach. I've had better times at the dentist. The atmosphere is tense. All attempts at fun and humor feel contrived. My sister Sarah is in a twenty-eight-day rehab program in New Jersey. She is cross-addicted to painkillers and alcohol following several years of surgeries on her knees and jaw. Her first attempt at rehab was several months ago, at a hospital I recommended. It did not go well and she relapsed quickly. I am stuck in those very old feelings that surge in these family turmoils. I resent the constant attention to Sarah, like no one else is hurting. But with the anger comes the guilt. It's a terrible combination.

There are too many of us in this three-bedroom condominium. Usually the closeness and chaos is fun, especially when I know it is time-limited. But this year we aren't just bumping into one another. We are slamming up against one another. Five minutes after we arrive, Mark explodes at my mother. Something sparks it like kerosene. They blow apart with Priscilla, the peacemaker, in between. They escalate in anger until my mother starts crying, something that rarely happens. It is like watching an explosion in slow motion. The pieces fly apart, wide and high. It is scary and riveting at the same time. I want to run away, but my feet are cemented to the tile floor.

Keara and my niece Chelsea retreat to a bedroom. When I go to check on them, I find them lying on the double bed. Chelsea looks frightened. Keara looks angry. Keara pronounces in disgust, "This family is so screwed up." I can tell she is upset, so I don't correct or criticize her. It is hard to hear my own child label my family as screwed up. She refers to us as "a bunch of French poodles—very high strung."

"And what about Dad's family?" I ask challengingly.

"Oh, that's easy," she tells me. "The Depenbrocks are Labs."

I look at the unraveling of my family and I can say "Sarah," but that's not totally true. It's unraveling in a lot of different places. Certainly I'm not woven too tightly these days.

Where do you take the anger at your family? The pain at all the imperfection, the cruelty so perfectly packaged within easy conversation, the isolation despite the togetherness? I need to be separate from them right now. I am drowning in them, the air is running out, and I will suffocate if I don't run. But where? Inside myself is no great solace these days.

Priscilla, Rachel, and I make plans to visit Sarah at the rehab center. Sarah has reluctantly agreed to see us, but does not want my parents to visit. My parents are beside themselves with a combination of grief, anger, confusion, and despair. I hope this visit will at least give us some reading on where she stands, with the drugs and the family.

July 7, 1990

I slip out of the condo for a blissfully solitary walk along the ocean. My march along the beach works off the tension of the family-packed condo. But there is also a pervasive dread that I can't pin on this trip. It's been there for a while. Psychologists call it "free-floating" anxiety. What contradictory words. Anxiety doesn't free-float. It stalks. It attacks. It lands on you with a thud.

The beach is shrouded in a gray mist, with the hard wind and angry waves blowing foam across the sand. I watch the fearless little sandpipers tease the tide like it is any gentle normal day. They always dodge the waves just in time, somehow managing not to get blown off course by this amazing wind. They make it look easy, almost fun. Undaunted, they keep playing, singly and in groups, oblivious to the fact that they are dancing with danger.

July 9, 1990

We start out early for Sarah's rehab center in New Jersey, hoping to beat the traffic. I spent last night at Rachel's. She is annoyed with me already because I coughed all night and because she could hear me pacing her small apartment in my insomnia. Even dreading the destination, we enjoy the trip. Rachel complains about how fast Priscilla drives. Priscilla complains about Rachel's complaining. As far as I'm concerned, they're both right. We alternately laugh, get serious, and then silent—each of us lapsing into our own anxieties about the visit. My father has constructed an elaborate set of directions for the best route, complete with intricate descriptions of possible motels, good places to go to the bathroom, and the populations of the towns we will be passing through. I guess we all manage our anxiety differently.

We stop at an old-fashioned country store and have a field day discovering the candy of our childhood—long strings of red and black licorice, Pez, smarties, and fireballs—followed by a heated debate about the relative merits of each kind. When we cross the state line, Rachel pops in a tape of Bruce Springsteen, the patron saint of New Jersey. We trade our candy and belt out the tunes with Bruce, liberally criticizing each other's voices.

We pull into a long driveway that leads to an imposing building. It is an old monastery converted into a rehab center. There is a definite prison feel to it. They search our bags at the door. I am relieved that I had the foresight to leave my drug-filled purse in the car. They assemble us in a huge room dotted with tables and chairs. A staff member introduces himself and outlines the routine for visiting hours. He asks all the "first-timers" to stand. Priscilla, Rachel, and I attempt to make a furtive collective decision, clearly wishing to remain invisible. We are not particularly successful at it. Priscilla begins to stand, but sees that we aren't and sits back down. Feeling guilty about Priscilla, I stand up, but she's already back in her seat. Rachel makes similar ambivalent and poorly timed moves. We look like the Three Stooges. Finally we get it together and stand simultaneously. I am praying that we don't have to make some kind of AA statement, like "My name is Martha and I am a codependent," or whatever the newest term is for having a lot of drug addicts and alcoholics in your family. The staff member welcomes us. Before we are allowed to see our relatives, all first-timers have to view a video on alcoholism. They lead us into a small, poorly ventilated room. Rachel, Priscilla, and I scrunch together on a couch that is supposed to look like leather but is really plastic and makes your sweaty legs stick to it. The video is long and boring as hell, complete with graphs and tables. My bronchitis and asthma keep me suppressing coughs constantly. But with all the talk about drugs and addiction I am too embarrassed to pull out my inhaler and take a few drags.

After our education, we are led back down to the orientation room to meet our relatives. I am unprepared for the flood of emotion I experience seeing Sarah walk into the room. She is in a knee cast and limping badly from a recent fall. She looks very thin, almost frail. Up close her face is uneven from the nerve damage of her jaw surgery. Her mouth droops somewhat, along with her left eye. As I hug her, I am surprised to be overcome with tears at seeing her and just being glad that she's still alive.

The first few minutes are very polite—denial in full tilt. But as the visit progresses I know that nothing has changed. She begins to tell me pointedly how this place is so much better than the place I had recommended. She says, "I went in there sane and came out insane." I will never be forgiven for that. She rails against my parents. Rachel is storming at this point, her face so cloudy I'm not sure what will happen. Sarah asks about the annual family trip to the beach. Priscilla answers honestly that it was intense, that everyone was on edge, and that there was a fair amount of conflict. The conversation starts to heat up slowly until I know for sure that we are on the way down. Rachel's tolerance for parent-bashing wears thin. She blurts out, "I am so angry at you, Sarah." Sarah can't tolerate this show of emotion, telling Rachel that she won't be blamed for Rachel's alcoholism and orders her to leave. Rachel runs out of the building in tears.

In my preachy oldest-child voice, I tell Sarah that she can't leave things like that with Rachel. That I don't expect them to kiss and make up, but I expect her to give Rachel a decent good-bye. She agrees and I go to look for Rachel.

I find her leaning against the hood of Priscilla's car, sobbing. A mangy mutt stands at her feet, barking insistently at her. It hurts me to see my baby sister in so much pain, feeling the responsibility of protecting my parents, who can take care of themselves. I kneel on the ground and hold her. We cry together. She fears that she has ruined the visit. I tell her that she was just the one who was most honest, and that eventually the charade would have crumbled anyway. She finishes crying and we return to the room. Priscilla is sitting alone in a circle of empty chairs. While we were gone, she and Sarah got into it and Sarah stormed out.

Here we are, in this huge room dotted with clusters of patients and their families. There is no one to talk to, no one to mediate. Sarah is just gone. We sit there for a few minutes, in case she has second thoughts and decides to return. She doesn't. We gather up our stuff and head out. The damn video was longer than the visit.

Even though we had planned to stay over at a motel, we decide unanimously that we want to get out of the state of New Jersey as quickly as possible. On the long ride home, we cry, then bitch, and then begin to laugh—about the mangy mutt barking at Rachel, about Rachel wanting to punch me during the video as she felt me suppressing my annoying coughs, about Priscilla feeling like a real jerk sitting there by herself after Sarah blew out. Priscilla drives too fast, but this time Rachel doesn't complain. We can't wait to finish with the "trip to hell."

July 10, 1990

We are fooling with medicines again. I feel like a science project. A little of this, a touch of that, and maybe we'll make me right again. I long to be right again. I long to wake up in the morning in anticipation rather than dread. To laugh for real at silly things. To run from one thing to the next like a hyperactive child, my old energy to be counted on whenever. I long to be a loving wife and mother. A good friend. I wait for work that will wake me up, keep me thinking and reaching, easing the burden of always listening to people in pain. It is toxic, this work, rubbing off and hurting me so badly, enveloping me in a fog of sad and frightened feelings.

How can I possibly be helping people? If only I had something else, they'd be sure to see it. Like a person with a broken leg consulting an orthopedist in a full body cast. But my patients seem satisfied with their care. Some of them are actually getting better. When I talk with their psychiatrists, they tell me that they think the therapy is going well. And the referrals keep coming in. Are these people blind? Kay assures me that many severely depressed people can reach way down inside themselves and pull out whatever they need to keep going. She tells me about highly accomplished people who, after their depressions, can't believe what they actually accomplished when they were in terrible shape. How do people do it? Perhaps they just narrow the field. Where once there was unlimited energy for many people and projects, now it is reserved and rationed carefully. Whatever energy I have goes to Keara and my patients. Even Brian has joined the waiting list.

July 12, 1990

After some terrific improvement with a new medicine, the bottom has dropped out again. Lew has me on a different medicine that is making me horribly nauseated. I have to interrupt a patient in the midst of discussing her revulsion at her recent sexual activity with an abrupt, "Excuse me for a moment." I run down the hall and get to the toilet just in time to retch my guts out. What timing. I'll even take this nausea if it will rid me of the dead feeling that leaves me listless and empty.

July 13, 1990

My sessions with Lew are an exercise in mutual discouragement. He is trying everything he knows and nothing is working. Now, not only do I feel like a lousy therapist, I feel like a lousy patient. I try to tell him how withdrawn I am becoming. I should come with a consumer warning, like the labels that say

"Handle with care" or "May be hazardous to your health." I am unfit for human consumption. I struggle to articulate how awful and isolating this feels, but I can't find the words. He looks me in the eye and says pensively, "You feel like a turd in the punchbowl."

I know now what I've suspected for some time. He knows this territory, not only as a tour guide, but as a native.

Nothing more is said. It doesn't have to be.

July 14, 1990

The boy next to me reads the airsickness bag in excruciating detail. I lean as far as I can into the aisle. He asks if I taught him third grade. I tell him I didn't. He asks me if I'm sure. I tell him I am. He makes remarks to the air, breathing in my direction. I try to read, hoping to extinguish this interaction. Back and forth we play the game: "Can I engage you?" "No, you cannot." But of course he does. He finally changes seats with a girl who copies her entire address book over. Exactly the same. No one gets added. No one gets dropped.

I read about people who have captivating conversations in transit. I always get the needy kids or sick old ladies. Of course, the people who sit next to me probably lament the luck of the draw that landed them with a cranky woman in short hair and long skirts who hides behind poetry magazines and offers only tight-lipped don't-expect-anything-from-me smiles.

We are on our way to Montana to visit our friends Tom and Louise. We will spend one week with them and another week in our own place on Flathead Lake. I have alternately looked forward to and dreaded this trip in the way I do before all vacations. Lew likened me to a barnacle. It is an apt metaphor. Tearing me loose from the pier is always traumatic, especially having to go so far for so long. People have commented that they think the change will "do me good." I'm not so sure. My life is so shaky that I cling to structure. I find comfort in the drastic curtailment of the social life that used to give me such pleasure. I shrink from the ring of the phone and the knock at the door. I am worried about being with other people. Of having to "fake it" for extended periods of time.

July 15, 1990

Montana is splendid. Clear weather, mountains and lakes. Tom and Louise's house is a riot of flowers and berries. They are wonderful hosts, making sinful strawberry daiquiris, fresh raspberry pies, and lists of plans. With his wicked sense of humor, Tom is quick to show us the front page of the local paper, which graphically outlines a grizzly-bear mauling very near where they plan to take us hiking in Glacier National Park. Hiking is one of the last things I want to do on this trip. Hiking in the company of hungry bears does nothing to heighten my desire.

Even in the midst of this breathtaking place and these dear friends, I feel anxious and tremendously out of place. I find it difficult to settle into someone else's rhythm and routine. To lose the privacy, the retreat to which I can escape and collapse.

July 16, 1990

I've begun settling into my own schedule. Mornings are
the worst. I am anxious and out of sorts. This is my vacation
and I count out the days like I'm working off a prison sentence.
My concentration is so bad that reading has become difficult. I
try to focus on an activity, take a walk, even clean something if
I have to. I push myself to try everything that is suggested:
white-water rafting, windsurfing, tubing, and skiing. With each
new activity, I wait for the jolt, the shot in the arm that will cat-
apult me out of this rut. The continuous editorial commentary
in my brain says, "This is wonderful. You've always wanted to
do this, stupid. Enjoy it." But the circuits must be blown, because the message never reaches the destination where pleasure
is experienced.

Tom and Louise arrange for a few hours of trail riding on
horseback to prepare us for the riding and hiking we'll be doing
in Glacier. I don't know if it is the horse or the trail, but ten
minutes into the ride my eyes start to water, my skin itches, and
I begin sneezing like a maniac. From the head of the line, Tom
sends down a wrinkled handkerchief that gets passed hand
over hand until it reaches me. My horse begins to slow down.
Every now and then, she comes to a complete stop, shakes her
head, and makes a horrific noise accompanied by a good jolt in
the saddle.

"What the hell is she doing?" I ask our guide with alarm.

"Oh," he tells me, "don't worry. She's just allergic. There's
something on this trail that really bothers her."

Those disgusting noises are apparently the horse equiva-
lents of sneezing, throat clearing, and nose blowing. My horse
and I plod along. We are a perfect match: irritated, miserable,
and slow. Each time she sneezes, some smart-ass up front yells,

"God bless you, Martha." I can't believe we're scheduled to do this for an entire day. The other riders are effusive in their appreciation as the guide points out some mountain, creek, or interesting plant.

I know it's beautiful and everything, but to be perfectly honest, I hate nature. And with my itchy face, swollen nose, bloodshot eyes, and wheezing lungs, I'm pretty sure the feelings are mutual.

July 17, 1990

Tom and Louise take one look at the shoes we plan to wear on our hike into Glacier and pronounce them absolutely unacceptable. We go to a store that sells things to rugged people who like to have intense and difficult encounters with the outdoors. An alarmingly healthy young man asks if he can be of assistance. I tell him I'd like one pair of size 7½ hiking boots.

"What kind?"

"What kind?" I repeat. I have the idea that hiking boots are basically generic items like those ugly orange waterproof ponchos or those basic metal water canteens. He points with pride to an entire wall of hiking boots and asks me what kind of hiking I'm planning to do.

"Well, you know, the kind of hiking where you walk up a mountain," I reply.

He leans over so as not to embarrass me and whispers confidentially, "This your first time?"

"Yes, Einstein," I think to myself. "What gave it away?" I nod humbly.

He nods back, reflects for a moment, and concludes with approval, "Cool." He is clearly excited to have a new recruit. "Where are you going?" he asks as he scans the boots.

"Glacier," I tell him.

Apparently this is another generic answer that leaves him totally dissatisfied.

"Where in Glacier?" he asks.

"I don't know. I'm just going to follow my friends."

He thinks about it for a moment. "That's cool," he says. "You're gonna love it. And the bears aren't too bad right now."

I manage a forced smile. He launches into a lengthy description of the relative merits of each brand of hiking boot. I hate to interrupt his spiel, but I finally tell him to just give me the cheapest ones. He warns me that the cheapos will not wear well "over the long haul." I assure him that there will be no long haul, that this will be the first and only time I wear these boots. By the look on his face you would have thought I was a virgin announcing that this is the first and only time I am ever having sex. He assesses me accurately as a lost cause, nods his head, and responds with his generic "That's cool." What he really means is "That's stupid," but I don't care.

I sit down to try on the boots. It takes him forever to lace them. He insists that I try them on with real hiking socks, which are just heavier, itchier, and uglier than the ones I'm wearing. I stuff my feet into the socks and the boots. They fit. I tell him he's got a sale.

"No, you have to walk around in them," he insists.

Just what I need. A salesman with integrity. I stand up and step off the six-inch platform where the shoes are displayed. The hard ridged rubber sole of my right boot snags a bit on the carpet. I turn my ankle. It hurts like hell, but I'm not about to admit it. He tells me I'm "favoring" my left side when I walk. I assure him that I always do that. He concludes the sale with obvious reservations.

Brian and I rendezvous at the main counter. He proudly displays his expensive, state-of-the-art hiking boots. I tell how I hurt my ankle.

"You hurt your ankle trying on hiking boots?" he asks loudly.

Louise, a physician, between fits of laughter promises to take a look at it when we get home. By the time we get back, my ankle is swollen and already bruising. The mortification of the manner in which I have injured myself is more than compensated for by the fact that now I have a valid "doctor's excuse" to sit out the hike.

Brian insists that it's the first psychosomatic sprained ankle he's ever seen. It is a perverse relief to have a " real," visible hurt. A hurt that people can recognize and understand. They wince in sympathy and know just what to do and what not to do. People can deal with this kind of pain. It all makes sense.

July 21, 1990

We're still on vacation. It is endless. We are now in an idyllic cabin in the middle of nowhere. For me, it is the equivalent of a "white room," "quiet room," "seclusion," "isolation," "time-out," and any other euphemism for being locked in a room totally devoid of stimuli. In other times, I would have found this restful. But in the total quiet, there is nothing to counteract the chaos inside me, the pain that reverberates more strongly because nothing balances it from the outside.

Brian and I sit alone on the dock. He is restless in his chair. When I ask what's wrong, he shrugs off the question.

Suddenly, he spots a black bear around the curve of the cove. It is on its hind legs, picking blackberries from a huge bush. Brian is thrilled, grabs his field glasses, and delivers a commentary on the bear's appearance and movements. He thrusts the field glasses at me with excitement. I take a cursory peek and hand them back. He looks incredulous and yells, "Damn it, Martha. That's a big black bear!"

I can't understand his anger and reply sheepishly, "The way I feel, Brian, it might as well be a big black bug."

He slams down the field glasses. "Doesn't *anything* move you?" he asks despairingly.

I don't know how to answer the question. Several moments of strained silence pass between us.

"I know this is hard for you, Brian," I say, trying to break the deadlock.

"No, Martha. I don't think you do. I don't think you know what it's like to have to manage everything alone. Keara, the house, the families, the friends. I dread calling you. I dread coming home to you because I don't know how you'll be. You are receding every day. I'm living with a ghost. And I don't know how much longer I can take this."

"What do you want me to do, Brian? I take my medicine. I go to therapy. I say my prayers. Tell me what you want me to do. Please. Because right now it takes all I have just to breathe and move and be."

Brian's eyes fill up and his bottom lip quivers. He leans over to me and whispers hoarsely, "I know it, Marth, and it's breaking my heart."

We hold hands across the lounge chairs, inhaling each other's sorrow. The big black bear lumbers about in the distance, savoring the sun and the juicy blackberries.

July 30, 1990

Brian has been much more honest with me since we've been back. He doesn't bite his lip anymore and swallow what he feels. He says he misses the fun, the spontaneity. He says I don't initiate anything anymore. I wish I could say, "That insensitive son of a bitch. He's wrong." But I can't. It's enough just to speak when spoken to, to give some minimal reaction to a stimulus. But to actually be the stimulus doesn't even occur to me.

I look at other people and think, "He lives without meds. She does. What is wrong with me? Am I so biochemically screwed up, so neurotic, so narcissistically self-absorbed that every hour is an obstacle course for me?" I don't know, but this can't continue. I feel like I am dying. A slow torturous death. And the worst thing is that I'm taking other people along for the ride. But I swear, I don't know how to do it differently.

August 1, 1990

I find myself preoccupied with thoughts of death. In some moment of emptiness or pain, an image of dying comes to me: a car accident, a heart attack, a vicious and quick-killing disease. In the psychiatric vernacular these are called "passive thoughts of death." But in my mind these thoughts are quite active. Rather than feeling the revulsion and fear that would have resulted from thinking about these things several months ago, now I find them strangely comforting.

I would never kill myself intentionally. I couldn't do that to my family, my friends, to Brian and Keara. But to have fate step in and give me a shove, that's a different matter. Then I have the exit, without the guilt. I am ashamed of myself for thinking like this. But more than anything, I am frightened that it makes me feel so much better to think about it. Somehow it eases the terror, the sense that I am condemned eternally to this hell.

August 3, 1990

Our answering machine has joined the basement grave-yard of machines that in very short periods of time have become indifferent to our messages. Brian searches the newspaper ads for the good buys. I announce that I do not want to replace it, that I could do without the burden of receiving and answering people's calls. Without a moment's hesitation, Brian and Keara override my veto. Brian buys it, installs it, and tries to explain the basic functions to me. I pretend to listen but comprehend and retain nothing.

He leaves very early this morning for work. There is a note on the dining room table telling me to leave a message for him using the Memo button on the new machine, so that he can call in and see how I'm doing.

I feel like shit, get dressed, and force down half a piece of toast. With my briefcase and keys in hand, I remember his request. I press the button and leave a message in a pathetic voice, "Hi. I feel really awful. I didn't sleep, so what else is new? I am so depressed. I don't know how I'm going to get through the day. I hate my life."

Two hours later, Brian leaves me a message on my office phone saying, "You have made a huge mistake. Call home." I dial my number, wait for the four rings before the machine kicks in, and prepare to hear Brian's voice announcing, "You have reached the Manning-Depenbrock residence. . . ." Instead, my own half-dead voice comes on the machine. "Hi. I feel really awful. I didn't sleep, so what else is new? . . . I hate my life." I press the remote. There are six messages, all hangups. I furiously dial Brian's number at work.

"Oh my God, what happened?"

"You must have hit the New Message button rather than the Memo button."

"Well, can't you change it?" I implore.

"I haven't learned how to change this one by remote yet and the manual is at home. Why don't you just run home and change it?"

"I'm booked solid for the next five hours. Jesus, I wonder who's called, who's going to call."

I spend the afternoon sitting and trying to listen to patients while wondering who is calling my house and hearing my pitiful message. So much for trying to keep my pain to myself. I might as well take out an ad in the *Washington Post*.

August 6, 1990

A four-year-old girl is referred to me for consultation. Her mother is dying, quickly. According to her parents, the child does not yet know. I introduce myself to Katy as someone who "helps kids with things they may be worried or scared about." She tells me she's not scared of anything. Knowing that words are rarely the best means of communicating with children, I invite her to play. From my large shelf of toys, she chooses the horses and says, "The big ones are the mommies and the little ones are their babies." She pretends the horses are at a rodeo, and no matter what happens, the black horse always wins, and knocks the babies down. The mothers try to protect their children, but they can't. The black horse comes in the night and steals the babies. The mothers try to fight him off, but they are killed in the process.

Katy places the kidnapped babies on a toy carousel. She spins it so hard that the babies fly off, landing all over the office. She repeats this sequence again and again, her laughter moving slowly from giggling to almost hysterical high-pitched shrieking. The ride goes faster and faster. The babies fall harder and harder. I ask with alarm, "What will happen to the babies?"

She shrugs me off and says stridently, "Well, some of 'em are just gonna have to die." She gives another anguished laugh and begins running around the room.

I pick up one of the fallen babies and hold it in my hand, stroking it gently. "They must be so frightened," I tell her.

Her running slows as she watches me pick up each baby. She comes closer to where I am sitting on the floor, and finally sits down next to me.

"Katy," I ask her, "do you think there is anyone who can help the babies?"

For the first time, her face registers pain and she whispers, "I don't know. Can *anyone* beat King Kong?"

August 7, 1990

Sugar, Keara's gerbil, is dying. Keara announces it at dinner and adds defiantly, "But I won't mourn her." When I ask why, she says, "She's already past her life expectancy."

I tell her, "Honey, so is Great-grandmother, but I'll mourn her when she's gone."

"Yeah," she counters, "but gerbils don't do anything special."

We look in the cage where Sugar and her daughter, Jania, live. Jania is begging for attention. Sugar looks at her with heavy eyelids. She tries to drag her hind legs a few millimeters, without success. Jania almost torments her mother, desperately trying to get her to move, to nudge her back into life. We watch in silence.

Without taking her eyes off the struggle, Keara asks, "Do you think she knows?"

August 18, 1990

Today is my thirty-eighth birthday. If only I had known a year ago what I would be facing now. Until last year I lived with the innocent arrogance that my life was the simple product of effort, will, and design. But now I am a house of cards, held precariously by the fragile conspiracy of wind, weight, and angle. Perhaps it is best that we cannot see into our futures.

Brian and Keara present me with lovely gifts, carefully chosen and shared. Brian lights the candles on my cake. As I close my eyes to blow them out, Keara prompts, "Make a wish, Mom."

A wish. What is a wish? A belief that thinking about something hard enough will make it happen?

When I was eight, I wished for a Cinderella watch, with the beautiful picture of her on the face and the exquisite pink band. It came in a glass slipper. Thoughts of that watch kept me awake at night in the days before my birthday. I got the watch, sure that the power of my wishes had made the dream come true. But to my great disappointment, the slipper was plastic, not glass. And from that moment on, making wishes was never the same.

My parents don't send me one of their usual cards, the kind my mother recycles from other people's birthdays. This time, it is a letter, written in my mother's hand. I begin to read it to myself, but Brian and Keara feel left out and protest, "No fair, read it out loud." I begin to read:

> Thirty-eight years ago you made a very difficult entrance into the world, looking very red, with no nose and a forceps cut on your cheek. Yours has always been a hard road, right from the beginning. Life has always demanded a lot of you and you have always responded with courage and acceptance. We applaud the spirit that keeps you going in good times and in bad. We are awed by your stubborn determination and are proud to be your parents. We love you deeply, Martha Mary Manning.
>
> Happy Birthday,
Mother and Dad

The tears come so fast I can hardly see the paper. I look at the gifts scattered across the table, the pile of cards, the remains of the cake. I hold my parents' letter to my chest. Gazing into the faces of my husband and daughter, I realize that if love were the cure, I would have been healed a long time ago.

September 3, 1990

Today is the last day of summer. What a time. What a long lonely time. I never knew the days could stretch out so endlessly. Stretch so far I think they'll break, but they only heave and sag. The weight of them bears down on me mercilessly. I wake after only two hours' sleep, into another day of dread. Dread with no name or face. Nothing to fight with my body or wits. Just a gnawing gripping fear. So hard and heavy. I can't breathe. I can't swallow.

The emptiness of the depression turns to grief, then to numbness and back again. My world is filled with underwater voices, people, lists of things to do. They gurgle and dart in and out of my vision and reach. But they are so fast and slippery that I can never keep up. Every inch of me aches. I can't believe that a person can hurt this bad and still breathe. All escapes are illusory—distractions, sleep, drugs, doctors, answers, hope. . . .

September 6, 1990

I want to die. I can't believe I feel like this. But it's the strongest feeling I know right now, stronger than hope, or faith, or even love. The aching relentlessness of this depression is becoming unbearable. The thoughts of suicide are becoming intrusive. It's not that I want to die. It's that I'm not sure I can live like this anymore.

I was always taught that suicide is a hostile act, suggesting anger at the self or at others. I have certainly seen cases in which this was true. Suicide was a final retribution, the ultimate "last word" in an ongoing argument. But I think that explanation excludes the most important factor—suicide is an end to the pain, the agony of despair, the slow slide into disaster, so private, but as devastating as any other "act of God." I don't want to die because I hate myself. I want to die because, on some level, I love myself enough to have compassion for this suffering and to want to see it end. Like the spy with the cyanide capsule tucked in a secret pocket, I comfort myself with the thought that if this ordeal gets beyond bearing, there is a release from it all.

I think about how to do it. I probably have enough pills in this house to kill myself ten times over. But with my sensitivities to medicines, I'm afraid I'd throw up, or only lapse into a coma, and be a further burden to Brian and Keara. If I do it, it must be final, no mistakes. I'm thinking about guns, wondering if I could actually check into a motel room and pull the trigger. As I come right up close to that image, I see Brian and Keara, their loss and anger and pain. And then I cry. Because I know that I am truly trapped. There is no escape. I cannot leave my child. A bad mother is better than a dead mother. But even knowing that, these thoughts, they won't leave me alone.

I try to pray when they come to me. But my own prayers are no match for them. In the middle of the night, I fumble around in the dark to find my grandmother's rosary beads at the back of my top drawer. I was so moved when she gave them to me. Smooth brown sandalwood, with a silver cross and the miraculous medal of the Blessed Virgin, with its inscription, "O, Mary, conceived without sin, pray for us who have recourse to thee." They were on the table by her bed. When I admired them, she picked them up and placed them in my hand, saying, "Take them, Maaahs Mary," her nickname for me. I told her that I wasn't really "into" the rosary. She insisted I take them anyway. I stuck them away in the back of a drawer, a piece of religious memorabilia, collectible like old baseball cards or bottle caps.

But no longer are these beads some entry in a spiritual scrapbook whose contents I largely reject. They are a lifeline. I roll the beads around in my hand, feeling a connection to my grandmother. In the middle of how many nights did she hold them, hoping that with each bead completed she might inch further toward relief, peace, grace? Guided by unconscious memory, I begin. I make the sign of the cross with the crucifix and place it to my lips. I pray the prayers long quiet on my tongue, but so easily retrieved. The recitation is a continual battle between despair and hope, death and life. The thoughts of guns and ropes and pills keep coming. I close my eyes to them, trying to squeeze them out of awareness.

Hail Mary, full of grace . . .

Block out the thoughts, Martha. Shut out the pain.

The Lord is with thee . . .

I can't do this. I can't go on.

Blessed art thou among women . . .

Please, just let me die.

And blessed is the fruit of thy womb, Jesus.

Jesus, where are you?

Keep going. Through the Hail Marys and the Our Fathers and the Glory Be's. Just say the words. Just keep saying them. Over and over and over again. Till the prayers find their way to heaven and I am blessed, finally, with the mercy of sleep.

September 8, 1990

With our combined vacations, I haven't seen Kay in almost a month. My deterioration is obvious to her. She tells me that I need "to consider ECT."

"ECT?" my mind screams. "Electroconvulsive therapy? Shock therapy?" I flash to scenes of *One Flew Over the Cuckoo's Nest,* with McMurphy and the Chief jolted with electroshock, their bodies flailing with each jolt.

She emphasizes the severity of this melancholic depression and reminds me that ECT has by far the highest success rate in this area. I feel like she has just told me I'm a terminal case. A lost cause.

She gives me literature to read about it. She reassures me that she is not giving up on the psychotherapy, but that she believes my suffering is mostly biological and has to be addressed. "Just think about getting a consultation," she encourages.

I nod, but I have absolutely no intention of doing so. I counter her concerns with a mental list of my admittedly dubious accomplishments. I still work. I still drive. I make my daughter's lunch. I pick her up from school. I answer the phone. How bad can I be?

As if sensing my silent resistance, she says, "If it was just a matter of personal strength and determination, you'd be fine. But it's not. You have to think of this as a serious illness. One that is potentially life-threatening."

When I get to the car, my hands tremble as I skim the pages of the literature she's given me. One is a recent National Institute of Mental Health consensus report that is highly favorable toward ECT for use in depressions such as mine. The side effects are scary, particularly the confusion and memory loss. Another article cites a study in which a majority of ECT patients reported that it was no more distressing than "a dental procedure." Always the empiricist, I wonder what choices were offered to the participants. "Was ECT more like having your eyes plucked out by vultures, or undergoing a simple dental procedure?"

When I tell Brian, he looks similarly horrified. "There must be other things that can be tried," he protests.

"She said she thinks I'm past the point where any medicine is going to pull me out. The ECT is not a 'cure' for depression, but somehow it's supposed to 'reset the clock,'" I tell him, trying to remember all the things Kay told me. "She said that you can call her or make an appointment to talk about it."

"Let's wait and see what Lew says when he gets back from vacation next week," Brian offers. "Maybe there is some other medicine. . . . Some other chance."

September 10, 1990

It's so hard to know when to hold on and when to let go. How much longer do we keep trying with new medicines? When do I finally "give in" and consider ECT? I've never been good at letting go. I've always figured that if I held on hard enough and long enough, I would eventually prevail.

When I was seven, I watched enviously as the bigger kids took their turns water-skiing. It looked so exciting, flying across the water, defying gravity with balance and speed. I pestered the big guys so long that they finally let me try. I slid my feet into the skis. Even at the smallest adjustment, I could feel myself slipping on the wet rubber, but I insisted that the fit was perfect. The boys walked me out into the freezing water, positioning me with my knees bent into my chest and my long skis facing up to the sky. It took the boat a while to circle back to shore. They fooled with the towline, trying to get it untangled. I was shivering, but determined. They handed me the towrope and instructed me to hold on hard. I gripped the handle, and a boy yelled, "Hit it." The boat lurched forward.

Instantly, I flew out of the skis. But I kept holding on to the towrope. I trailed the speeding boat, ingesting salt water by the mouthful. I was totally disoriented, but thought I heard voices calling to me from the shore. I raised my head out of the water and could slowly decipher what they were yelling, "Martha, let go of the towrope. Let it go!" It took several moments to register the

meaning of what they were saying. Finally, I loosened my grip
and watched the boat speed away with the towrope bobbing and
dancing in its wake, just as I'd been doing seconds before. I rested
in the water, allowing my life jacket to do all the work, cursing
my small feet, and shaking with fear and cold.

I think of that image often these days: the frigid water, the brief flight, my arms almost ripped from their sockets but still stubbornly holding on to that damn rope for dear life. The same rope that was causing me such pain. Beyond strength, beyond safety, beyond good sense. I hear those voices in the distance, the voices I so rarely heed, yelling, "Let go, Martha. Just let go." I want to do as they say. But there's a part of me that fears now, just as I did then, that if I let go, I will surely drown.

September 12, 1990

I sit on the couch in the hall at Lew's office waiting for my first appointment since his vacation. His ocean-machine reminds me of the beach in autumn. The days still hold the summer's warmth, but the nights begin their surrender to winter. The beach is emptied of all people and noise; there's just the ocean and the gulls. The rhythm of the waves is hypnotic and endlessly reassuring. Still the gentlest lullaby I know. I wish I could put that in a capsule to swallow at night.

Lew takes one look at me and says that he doesn't even need to ask how I'm doing. I pour it all out to him: I can't sleep. I can't eat. I can't read or talk or concentrate for more than several seconds. The force of gravity around me has tripled. It takes so much effort just to lift an arm or take a step. When I am not curled up in a ball on the couch, I pace. I rock desperately in my rocking chair. I wring my hands.

"What about suicide?" he asks gently.

I tell him that every morning, in the window between asleep and awake, for a moment I feel okay, like it's all been only a nightmare. But then I open my eyes and recognize my room. I realize who and where I am. And every morning I utter the same lament, "Oh God, I'm still alive."

"Have you been thinking of suicide?" he asks, pushing me to be more direct.

I look away from him and fix my eyes on the leg of a chair. "Yes," I confess. "Sometimes." *Please,* I'm thinking, *please don't make me get specific. Please don't make me spell it out.* But the psychologist in me knows he can't dance around this one.

"What do you imagine when you think about it?" he asks.

"I think about pills, but I'm afraid I'd botch the job. I've thought about hanging. I think I know the basics of it, but I'm afraid I could screw that up too. Now I'm thinking about guns." I am mortified to be telling him this. More ashamed about this than anything I've ever said or done.

He is very calm with his questions. "What stops you?"

"Keara, I can't leave Keara. Brian is strong. Ultimately I know he'd be alright. But I can't do this to my child. She is the only thing that stands between me and dying."

"That's important, Martha. You have to hold on to that."

"But Lew, I'm so afraid. What if I lose even the connection to her?"

"Then you have to tell Brian and Kay and me." He concludes that he does not consider me at significant risk for suicide "right now," which is consistent with Brian's assessment. I promise him that I will not be silent with my despair. I feel greatly relieved to have spilled it out so graphically to someone. He doesn't rush to lock me up. He seems to understand what I'm saying on a basic and visceral level.

We discuss Kay's recommendation of ECT and my resistance to it. He wants to take one more shot at a new medicine, with the caveat that if it doesn't work, I will consider ECT. He encourages me to gather information about the doctors and hospitals who perform it, and perhaps even set up a consultation, "just in case."

September 13, 1990

The kitchen windowsill is littered with bottles of pills. Lovely party-pastels in circles and squares with strong vanquishing names like Prozac and Xanax. Or sweet promising ones like Halcion and Asendin. And all these potions make me big for a while, but the sweetness of their promises melts like kisses somewhere inside me. And I become small again. So small that I can't find myself. All I can find is my fear. The fear that my daylight is truly past and I am destined only for night.

September 22, 1990

I wake into panic, in the middle of a dream about suicide. It leaves me with a terrible hungover feeling I can't shake. I am afraid that the dream is a prediction. I try to go to my Saturday-morning meditation group. I park the car but almost turn back two or three times before I get to the front door. Clare presents a reading from the Sufi religion and she and Jeremy discuss it. I try to listen and add something, but I can hardly follow the conversation. I can't even fake it anymore.

At the break I excuse myself with a lie that I have to get to Keara's softball game. I know that I can't make it through forty-five minutes of silent meditation. I come home crying. More empty tears to God about why this is still happening. Tears for an end to it. Tears for mercy.

The house is deserted. I search for things to do. It is all I can do just to empty the dishwasher and sweep the floor. Then I lie on the couch and stare into space, vacant and deadened. I have a haircut appointment that I am already dreading, even though it's three hours away. How will I keep up a conversation with my effusive hairdresser? It will be a monumental effort just to move my lips into a smile. My face is simultaneously waxy and frozen. The muscles have gone on strike.

The infinity of this vacancy, the pervasive pain, the longing for some spirit, some lightness, some joy—that's all that is left.

I am afraid. Afraid of managing the desolation of each second. Afraid that I won't make it to the next hour. These feelings are still so alien to me. Time used to be something I loved to play with, to tease, to race. But there is no contest now. I envy Keara, her many new beginnings—school, dancing, softball. She gulps her cereal this morning. When I warn her to slow down, she protests, "I can't, Mom. The day is waiting for me!"

Depression is such a cruel punishment. There are no fevers, no rashes, no blood tests to send people scurrying in concern. Just the slow erosion of the self, as insidious as any cancer. And, like cancer, it is essentially a solitary experience. A room in hell with only your name on the door. I realize that every person, at some point, takes up residence in one or another of these rooms. But that realization offers no great comfort now.

When I invoke the continual lament, "Why me?" I remember what my friend Louise said as I cursed the unfairness of my first miscarriage. I cried to her, "Why did this have to happen? Why?" Because she is a physician, I expected some plausible and complicated medical explanation. But Louise is also a woman who has lost a baby. And out of that wisdom, she shrugged and said gently, "Because, Martha, it was just your turn."

September 30, 1990

Bad panic and depression. Try to fight the magnetic force field that pulls me toward the sanctuary of the bed or couch. See three patients. Can barely understand them.

October 2, 1990

Increase dose of medicine. Very groggy. Can't get started. Swim twenty laps. See four patients. Awful.

October 6, 1990

The thoughts of death and nothingness are like a fever I can't shake. What is the distance between the thought and the act? How far was it for my cousin between this feeling and the rope around her neck?

October 8, 1990

Slept one hour last night. I'm the first one at the pool, desperate for water to revive me. Each stroke is torture. I cry in the pool. I'm up against the limit of my endurance. I can't see patients today.

I think more about ECT. I'm scared about taking so much time off, losing all that money, the medical bills. The procedure scares me. The hospital scares me. Losing my memory scares me. So many parts of the body have a twin, or at least some potential for transplantation. But this is my brain. My one and only brain.

It has no counterpart. No backup.

October 11, 1990

I clench my hands constantly, wringing them in turmoil. I pace. I rock mechanically in my rocking chair. I lie curled up on the couch. I don't know what the next step is and it scares me. There are so many choices and no guarantees. My life is a field, booby-trapped with land mines. One could go off in a place least expected and leave me in even worse shape than I am right now. God, I wish there were an answer. I am so tired.

October 12, 1990

I am in bad shape. I call the local hospital to find the name of the doctor who does ECT. I am given the name of a Dr. Richard Samuel and the nurse says he is "very good." I'm never sure anymore what that actually means. People think I'm "very good" and I know how wrong they are. I dial the first few digits of his number and hang up. It takes me about six tries to complete the call. I set up an appointment for a consultation. He agrees to see me later today. I can't believe I'm actually doing this.

Brian and I meet with Dr. Samuel. He has already talked to Lew and has the basic information. I feel disoriented through much of the session. I have a hard time following the discussion.

It is as if he and Brian are talking and I am listening at the keyhole of a closed door.

He interviews me carefully about my symptoms. I don't sleep. I don't eat. I am slowed down, grinding toward a complete halt. I stare out into space. I feel like English is my second language. I am almost mute. I register a fraction of what goes on around me. I don't even think about suicide anymore because I'm sure that I'm already dying. I don't even have the energy to speed it up. He pronounces me "an excellent candidate." With remnants of my achievement obsession still intact, I almost thank him, like it's some kind of compliment. He gives us things to read about the procedure. Since I am not currently a major suicide risk, and since I have such a strong "support system," Dr. Samuel sees no reason for me to be in the hospital and explains that he can perform ECT on an outpatient basis. He tells Brian that someone will have to "take responsibility" for me since I am likely to get confused and forgetful. He will call us to set up the first treatment after he gets authorization from my insurance company.

October 13, 1990

My insurance company, in its infinite stupidity, declares that since I don't have outpatient mental health benefits, it will cover me only as an inpatient. We try to estimate with Dr. Samuel how much we will spend if we pay out-of-pocket to do it outpatient. He reminds us that the total cost will include not only his fee, but also fees for the anesthesiologist, recovery room, and nursing staff.

The biggest unknown in the equation is the number of treatments I will need. The lowest number is six, the highest twelve. The prospect of so much money staggers us, especially since we don't know when I will return to work. But I can't go into the hospital. I just can't. Dr. Samuel recommends that I at least visit the unit where I would stay. He promises to call ahead to let them know I'm coming.

I visit the unit. It looks recently redecorated—all mauves and greens in the style of a Holiday Inn. The assistant head nurse gives me a tour and asks how I have gotten so depressed. I stare at her blankly and can't find the words. She might as well ask me why I have brown hair or why I'm not taller. I tell her that I am mostly depressed about being depressed. Her expression informs me that this clearly is not the correct answer. I imagine the opening statement in my chart: "Patient demonstrates limited insight into her current problems." She says dubiously, "Dr. Samuel said you are a psychologist," as if somehow that should make me more articulate about my pain. I reply sheepishly that I am a psychologist but that I'm not very good, in the hope that this will explain any deficits in my clinical presentation.

A huge bulletin board in the nurses' station lists patients' names and privilege status. I freeze when I see my own name with the notation "Hold" in front of it. *Hold Manning*. I panic and can't quite catch my breath. I tear out of the place, through the double doors, down strange-smelling halls, and finally through an exit door. I climb into my car, lock all the doors, and try to calm myself. I resolve to avoid the hospital at all costs. I will handle my problems. It is a matter of determination. I will make it work. The most important thing is that I am free—to walk out, to drive home, and never to return.

Driving down my street, I pass a woman and her daughter stuffing scarecrows in their front yard. It is a cool bright yellow-orange kind of day and they are totally immersed in their creations. Their laughter is pure music and they are golden in their joy. I am seized with the most piercing sadness—that I have lost that capacity, for playing, for creating, for relishing beauty. I pull up in front of my own house and turn off the ignition. I lay my head against the steering wheel and my body shakes with wrenching sobs that have been contained for too long. I know now what I have to do. It is time. It is past time.

Another refrain from "Song in a Year of Catastrophe" comes to me:

> I let go of all holds then, and sank
> like a hopeless swimmer into the earth . . .

I try to remember the rest, but I can't.

When I was nine, I climbed up to the high diving board at Jones Beach for the first time. My initial enthusiasm was betrayed by a mounting fear the farther I progressed up the ladder. There were at least ten children behind me occupying their own rungs, impatiently waiting for their chance at flight. Turning back was not an option, so I flung myself off the board. The fall was so fierce, so sharp, that I was buried in water. I kept sinking lower and lower, the air bursting in my chest and the terror overtaking me. I was frightened that I would never come up, that there was no bottom to this pool. I "sank like a hopeless swimmer." But finally, finally, my big toe skimmed the jagged concrete floor of the pool. I flexed my foot and pushed off against the bottom, propelling myself upward, back to air and sun and life.

This memory comforts me somehow, though I don't know why.

October 14, 1990

It takes so much effort to pack, each piece of clothing a reminder of where I am going and how much I don't want to go there. I change the message on my office machine and talk to several patients with shreds of my "Dr. Manning" voice. My friend Ed agrees to cover my practice for me. He makes me tea in the mug I gave him for Christmas. We sit on the porch while he smokes a lot of cigarettes and helps me compose letters to my patients.

I sit next to him as he cranks them out on his computer. I love him for walking me through it and for not trying to make conversation. He does try one joke on me. "What did the Zen master say to the hot dog vendor? . . . Make me one with everything."

October 15, 1990

Brian has one of his long clinical days and with my practice out of commission for at least a month, we can't afford for him to miss a single hour. We stand with my packed bags around us. He holds me long and hard. In our twenty-two-year relationship we have never had a more painful good-bye.

My mother offers to take me to the hospital. She is preoccupied with thoughts of her own mother, who is quite depressed and having panic attacks at being alone. Talk about getting it from both sides. As soon as she gets me settled, she is flying to Boston to assess the situation.

My mother's usual dark Irish response to complaints of pain is to encourage you to think of someone worse off than yourself. Complain of a headache and she'll answer, "Oh, that reminds me, say a prayer for _____. She has a brain tumor." This time she offers no one who is worse off than I. Instead she says, "I spoke to Aunt Nancy last night and she said that she's remembering you in her prayers." In my family, when they're remembering you in their prayers, you know you're a goner.

It is excruciating to send Keara off to school, to close the door to my home and to my study and all the things that keep me tethered to the world. Checking into Admitting, I almost choke on the words "Psychiatric Unit." My mother chats her way through it, filling up the empty time and space with trivia that matters to neither of us, but keeping me engaged and stemming the tide of tears. As the admitting secretary types out the forms, I think to myself, "This is going to become part of my *permanent record.*" As a child I remember so many people in authority wielding that threat. When I was arrested for shoplifting with my friends at the age of fifteen, the policeman warned us that if we "kept our noses clean" for a year, our slates would be wiped clean and it would not become part of our "permanent record." There is no such reprieve here. Like losing your virginity, hospitalization for a psychiatric disorder involves crossing over a line that can never be erased.

We are met by Sharon, who introduces herself as my primary nurse. She takes a history, with my mother interjecting corrections to my memories of childhood surgeries and illnesses. Sharon inspects my purse and suitcase, taking inventory of my belongings and ferreting out all "sharps." Some things I immediately understand. All glass containers can be broken and used to cut, but tweezers? I try to imagine what it must be like to pluck yourself to death. I'm pleased that she doesn't find the three Xanax that I've stashed in the back compartment of my suitcase. I remember all those small pleasures at getting away with things that fueled my adolescence. It is demoralizing to have someone go through my things like this, but I guess that it is only the first of many assaults on my autonomy.

Sharon shows me to my dreary room. Right outside the only window is a brown trailer used for the drug unit. It blocks out all sun. So far, I don't have a roommate. My mother unpacks my things and organizes the tiny closet as I sit on the bed crying. Until this week I have been too depressed even to cry, and now I can't stop. She asks me to make a list of things I'd like her to get before she leaves. I can't think of anything, so she tells me she'll use her imagination. She returns shortly with several six-packs of Diet Coke and refrains from her usual lecture about my lousy nutrition. She hands me several pads of paper and a package of pens, reminding me that it was at the lowest point in her life that she began to paint. "No matter how bad you feel," she tells me, "you must keep writing."

After an hour she is encouraged by the nursing staff to leave so that I can "settle in." I feel like a little girl being left on her first day of school. I wish her luck with my grandmother and she sighs wearily, knowing the price that is always exacted from her by her mother.

After I pull myself together, I quickly figure out that the most important thing is to find out my "privileges." The concept of privileges on inpatient units has always irked me. Adults come onto a unit with a number of "rights," some of which must be curtailed for their own protection. However, I have often seen rights turned into privileges and conferred on people for compliance, rather than health. In the space of one hour, the right to set out walking whenever I please has become a privilege, something that must be bestowed upon me. How do I earn it? By behaving myself, spilling my guts, providing a shining example?

Each patient's privilege status is spelled out on a huge board in the nurses' station. There is nothing next to my name, and the nurse at the desk tells me I'll have to wait to see what Dr. Samuel decides. The highest privilege is "unaccompanied," which means that you can walk off the unit alone for thirty minutes at a time as long as you stay on hospital grounds. I am disheartened to see that not a single person has "unaccompanied," and I resolve to do major lobbying with Dr. Samuel on this point. I am already claustrophobic in this space. The freedom to walk will greatly enhance my sanity.

At dinner I get my first chance to check out the other patients. There are a great variety of people, with a surprising number of broken bones and bandaged wrists. Depressed people seem to be the most represented. There are a number of older women who barely move. One woman is in a wheelchair. She is on oxygen constantly, except when she smokes cigarettes. Another woman looks like she's had a stroke. She maligns her husband loudly as he tries to interest her in dinner and moans repeatedly, "Oh God, please take me." There is another woman who looks so familiar, but I can't place her. The manic and psychotic people appear to make the most interesting dinner companions. They fill in my oppressive silence with conversation that puts me at ease, even though I don't understand very much.

Dinner is served on nauseatingly pink trays. My appetite is definitely not helped by the presentation of food. The entire dinner is white: fish, rice, cauliflower, milk, and vanilla pudding.

I have no idea what to do with myself, and it's too early to go to bed. I sit on my bed, blankly staring into space. A basset hound walks past my door. I blink hard. Then two chihuahuas prance by. A loudspeaker announces that "pet therapy" is beginning in the lounge. Pet therapy? Jesus Christ, this is worse than I thought.

Having been told that there is a bathtub on the unit, I'm reassured that at least one nightly ritual can be continued. I search the women's bathroom, noting that the doors on the toilet stalls don't close entirely, and certainly don't lock. The mirror is a fake, made of aluminum rather than glass. I see my reflection, diffuse and distorted. I search out a nurse who leads me to a locked closet containing a bathtub. The water never gets beyond tepid, and I wonder if this too is purposeful. A scream pierces my solitude. It is coming from the other side of the closet. A man is thundering and pacing, enjoining all of us heathens to repent before it is too late. I deduce that the adjoining closet is a seclusion room, a place to keep people who are detained for acting overtly "crazy." While I miss the silence of my bath, I am engrossed in his ravings. I envy him his energy, and the righteousness of his rage. I wish I could feel his connection to the God who abandoned me so long ago.

October 16, 1990

I am still in disbelief that I am here. The night is eternal, interrupted every fifteen minutes by a nurse doing "checks" with an annoying flashlight. But even without the interruptions, I would not be sleeping. I take a walk around the unit at 2:00 A.M. The fluorescent lights in the hall and nurses' station give an eerie cast to the place. Many people are already up, silently walking the halls in bathrobes and pajamas. We look like ghosts, lost souls inhabiting the shells of our former selves, pacing and counting out the hours till daylight.

In the middle of the night I get a roommate. She is still asleep. I know nothing about her except that she is a cheerleader, because her uniform is the only thing hanging in her closet. Being a depressed cheerleader must be as tough as being a depressed therapist.

We are awakened each morning by loudspeaker. A nurse announces that the *Washington Post* is available for purchase at the nurses' station. We line up groggy and yawning to have what are left of our vital signs assessed by the staff. I run to the phone to call Brian. I get tearful talking to him and can sense his weariness over the phone.

My first ECT is scheduled for tomorrow morning. I am frightened because it sets me on a course from which I cannot turn back. More than losing my memory, I am terrified that I will lose the last remnants of myself.

Immediately after breakfast, I am summoned by loudspeaker to psychodrama group. It is 8:30. Most of us are fighting off a combination of too little sleep and too much medication. Now we are supposed to express our innermost feelings and conflicts through drama. Marie, the psychodrama therapist, is loose and warm. She wears cowboy boots, and on that basis I decide that I like her. However, I have a perverse desire to say that I will participate in this stuff when she shows me hard data on its efficacy in the treatment of severe depression. But I really want the "unaccompanied" privilege, and anyway, I'm too tired to make trouble.

Marie announces that there are two new people in the group. It is apparent who we are because we're the only two people crying. The other woman, Katherine, cut her wrists last night. She sobs and says how much she hates the place and wants to get out. Like newborns who cry in response to the wails of other babies, I burst into tears. Marie places a number of diverse objects in the middle of the room and asks us to choose the ones that most represent how we are feeling. I choose a bright red pillow with a STOP sign on it and a toy sailboat. She asks us to do something I have hated since my first day of kindergarten—"share." We have to go around the room and give the reasons we picked our objects. When my turn comes, I say something inane about wanting the depression to STOP, and wishing I could just sail away.

After psychodrama comes art therapy. Katherine and I are still sniffling. Denise, the art therapist, puts aside her agenda for the moment and allows the people in the group to talk to one another. Barbara tells us how she took an overdose after rounds of cancer chemotherapy and reassures us that she cried continually for a week when she found out that she was going to have to live.

Emmaline, a manager and mother of two girls, adds that she had problems with her lithium and got so high that she was convinced she was going to marry Michael Jordan. She landed in the hospital when she went so far as making the wedding arrangements. The crowning blow came when she modeled her new wedding gown for her husband and sons. She slaps her knee when she finishes her story and laughs so hard she shakes.

Denise invites us to use pastels to draw whatever we want. I draw a huge eye crying and write a poem next to it. Katherine leans over and says, "You don't have to tell me what you do. I know you're a writer." I am relieved not to have to tell people I'm a psychologist and nod my assent.

My friend Pat comes at lunchtime. She brings a painting from her daughter, Suzanne, with a note that says she hopes I'll "stop being sad." Pat sits on my bed while I cry all the tears that have been locked up inside me in the service of survival. She rubs my back as I rest my head on her shoulder.

After lunch I call Lew, who is scheduled to leave for a trip to Italy tomorrow. I let him know that my first treatment is scheduled for tomorrow morning. He has talked to Dr. Samuel and communicates his confidence in him. I wish him a good trip. He wishes me "courage."

It is rumbling and pouring down rain, echoing the mood on the unit. There is a kind of moral imperative on psychiatric units about keeping people occupied. We are divided into two groups. They call them Group 1 and Group 2, but just like in first grade, when you knew that the Red group were better readers than the Blue group, it doesn't take a Ph.D. to figure out how people are assigned. I am in the "high functioning" group, mostly depressed and manic-depressive people.

The next stop in the forced march is "support group," which is the worst so far. Two well-meaning nurses lead it and hand out the sappiest poems, which I'm sure are supposed to be inspirational. We are asked to reflect on them and then discuss them in small groups. It is like reading long greeting cards. The contrast between the mood of the group and the tone of the poems is totally wasted on the nurses, who are so perky and upbeat that I want to scream.

With every burst of thunder, I worry about how Keara is faring on her walk home from the bus stop. I wonder whether she has the right clothes and if she can really master the keys to the front door. I monopolize the patient phone anxiously dialing our number. When she finally answers, she delivers her daily complaint—she's "starving and there's nothing to eat." I lead her through a tour of the refrigerator and sit on the phone with her while she has her snack.

Dr. Samuel arrives to discuss tomorrow's ECT. He leads me to a conference room and bends over the lock, fiddling with his keys. I remember all the times patients waited at locked doors while I fumbled to open them. It is strange, now, to be on the other side of the keys. The kids at the hospital where I did my postdoctoral fellowship preferred to steal our keys over anything else in our briefcases or purses. They never used them to get in or out; they just taunted us with them, jiggling them in our faces. They understood that the keys were more than just a means of entry and exit. As young as they were, they knew that these were the keys to the kingdom, the passports to power, the difference between the keepers and the kept.

Dr. Samuel explains ECT one more time before I give my written consent. Tomorrow morning I will be awakened at 5:00 A.M. for a shot of atropine, used to dry secretions before many hospital procedures. I will change into a hospital gown and be wheeled down to a recovery room, where the treatments are administered. I will be attached to monitors that will register the activity of my heart and my brain. A band will be fastened around my head. Because I am having unilateral ECT, several electrodes will be placed over the temporal region of my non-dominant hemisphere. An oxygen mask will be placed over my nose and mouth. Through an IV, I will receive succinylcholine, which will immobilize me to prevent the breakage of bones, and methohexital, a short-acting anesthetic. Between 80 and 170 volts will be administered for between one-half and one second, inducing a grand mal seizure that will last for thirty to sixty-five seconds. I will awaken approximately fifteen to thirty minutes later. He warns that I may have a headache, confusion, and memory loss following the treatment.

I listen to this with the cool demeanor of a fellow professional. He asks if I have any questions and I tell him calmly that between the reading material he provided and our discussions, I feel prepared. However, on the inside I am screaming, "HOW DO I KNOW YOU'RE NOT GOING TO FRY MY BRAINS? WHAT IF THE MACHINE SHORT-CIRCUITS? WHAT IF YOUR HAND SLIPS AND YOU PUSH THE DIAL TOO FAR? WHAT IF I TOTALLY LOSE MY MEMORY? WHAT IF I DIE?" I conclude that he probably has no answers to these questions, so I spare him the hysteria. He hands me the forms to sign. My hand shakes as I take the pen. I talk to myself in my calmest, cut-the-bullshit voice. "The bottom line," I say to myself, "is that my life has already almost slipped away from me. I have two choices: I can end it or I can fight like hell to save it."

I write my name slowly and he signs as a witness. I'm scared right down to my shoes and wonder how I'll get through the night. He anticipates my concerns and offers a mild sedative to help me sleep. I tell him that over the past year we have tried every sedative, hypnotic, and tranquilizer known to medicine in doses that would knock out an Amazon for a week. None keeps me asleep for more than two hours. He gently reminds me that even two hours would be a vast improvement over what I'm getting now.

Brian and Keara come for their first visit. I cannot hold them enough. Keara surveys the unit and with her typical candor says, "Boy, Mom, I really feel sorry for you. I'd hate this place." She is fascinated with my roommate, Jennifer, whom she recognizes as several years ahead of her in school. She asks what Jennifer is "in for."

I reply sanctimoniously, "Keara, you know I can't tell you that."

She responds with dead aim. "Mom, she's not your patient. She's your roommate."

"Oh yeah," I answer, appropriately chagrined, "I guess she's depressed."

Keara is incredulous and protests, "How could she be depressed? She's beautiful!" I look at this alien being who greets each morning with a song and know that I'll never explain it to her satisfaction.

I show Brian the cafeteria. Terry, the woman I thought I recognized from someplace else, comes out of the smoking room at the same time. Brian, who never forgets a face, grabs my arm and asks, "Remember her?" I look at him like he's the one who should be the inpatient. "Sammy's," he hints. I draw a blank. Then he pretends to play the triangle and sings, "Fast car. . . ." It all comes back to me. I'm in the hospital with the woman who played a triangle and performed a Tracy Chapman number to the dismay and discomfort of the patrons at Sammy's Diner.

October 17, 1990

The night is interminable and I pace the halls again. At 4:30 someone tiptoes into my room with a flashlight and whispers that it's time for my shot. On the entire nursing staff there is one male and I have the good fortune to have him administer the shot in the butt. He leaves a hospital gown and fuzzy blue slippers and tells me to go to sleep for a while. But it's a lost cause. I hate the waiting and start to cry. Over and over, I repeat to myself the end of a Jane Kenyon poem called "Let Evening Come."

Let it come as it will, and don't
be afraid. God does not leave us
comfortless, so let evening come.

The day staff replaces the night staff. My nurse comes with a wheelchair. She must notice how frightened I am because she pats my shoulder and tells me everything will be alright. This small act of kindness makes my eyes fill up. Words stick in my throat. She wheels me through the long dark halls in silence.

The recovery room is all bright lights and shiny surfaces. There are eight beds, all empty. A group of people are assembled around a stretcher, which I assume is meant for me. Dr. Samuel introduces me to the team—two nurses and an anesthesiologist. They help me onto the stretcher and for a moment the anxiety about the ECT is replaced by the anxiety of having my bare ass visible through the open back of my hospital gown. While they uncross wires and plug in machines, I take a horizontal inventory of the room. In anticipation of Halloween it is decorated with orange and black crepe paper. Black rubber spiders and little skeletons are suspended from the ceiling. What were these people thinking?

I am covered with hands. They take hold of different parts of me, staking out their territory. Voices tell me this is a dance done hundreds of times before, so I need not be afraid. But their casual confidence, their ease with my body, gives me no comfort. Just as I have lost so much of myself in the past year, now I lose more. I offer myself up to these strangers in exchange for the possibility of deliverance. Someone holds my hand and slips needles under my skin. Another slides down my gown and plants red Valentine hearts on my chest. Fingers anoint my temples with cool ointment and fasten a plastic crown tightly around my head. Wires connect me to machines that hum and beep, registering the peaks and valleys of my brain and my heart. They cover my mouth and nose with plastic and instruct me to breathe. For several horrible seconds, I am paralyzed before I lose consciousness. This is the nightmare that has haunted me since I was a child. I am on a beach, caught between a tidal wave and a towering seawall. In my terror, I am frozen. I cannot run, or move, or scream. The waves slam me down and take me with them. I am drowning.

I open my eyes, squinting at the glaring white lights. A nurse smiles down and welcomes me back. She reports that I had a "good seizure," which as far as I'm concerned belongs

with other psychiatric oxymorons like "uncomplicated be-
reavement" and "drug holiday." My head hurts and my jaw is
sore. A nurse from the psychiatric unit picks me up several
minutes later and delivers the best news I've had in a while. I
am excused from all group activities on the days I have ECT.

My father comes for his first visit. He does his typical
challenge of the nurse's authority when she tries to rifle
through the things he has brought. I get vicarious pleasure
from watching the retired FBI agent resist a search. He brings all
kinds of goodies, which he produces one at a time, searching
my face for approval. He lends me his Walkman and a tape of
John Philip Sousa marches. In another bag are ten legal pads,
ten pens, and a box of chocolate-covered cherries. I can tell
how uncomfortable he is visiting his daughter on a psychiatric
unit. If my mother were here, she'd be doing all the talking and
he'd be standing around looking restless.

He surveys my miserable room and asks, "Can you go for
a walk?" When I nod, he mutters, "Let's get the hell out of here."

We walk around the perimeter of the hospital. It is a gor-
geous autumn day, the color of fire. The cool air against my
skin is the perfect antidote for the anesthesia still lingering in
my system. My father asks endless questions, "So, are you alright? Are you sure you're warm enough? Are you getting
enough to eat?" He asks all the questions except the ones he'd
most like to ask, "Why are you so depressed?" and "What did we
do wrong?"

The day is filled with visits from brothers, sisters, and
friends. Flowers and cards pile up on the windowsill. Knowing
my lust for reading, everyone comes bearing books. I try to
thank them enthusiastically, hoping that someday I will have
enough concentration to actually read them. A messenger delivers a book from Kay. It is about the Washington National

Cathedral. Inside she has inscribed a portion of T. S. Eliot's *Murder in the Cathedral.*

> We praise Thee, O God, for Thy glory displayed in
> all the creatures of the earth,
> In the snow, in the rain, in the wind, in the storm;
> in all of Thy creatures, both the hunters
> and the hunted.
> For all things exist only as seen by Thee, only
> as known by Thee, all things exist
> Only in Thy light, and Thy glory is declared
> even in that which denies Thee; the
> darkness declares the glory of light.

A nurse suggests that I record my gifts because I might not be able to remember them later. I give her one of my "What a good idea, but I have no intention of doing it" smiles. Like I'm really going to forget something as simple as the gifts people gave me.

Keara runs down the hall toward me and calls proudly, "Guess what? Carrie's mother was in the hospital for depression too." I put on my best impassive psychologist face to mask the fact that I am totally taken aback. Brian, who hasn't even told his family, stiffens. I try to ask casually,

"Oh, how did that come up?"

She looks absolutely thrilled with herself and answers, "We talked about it in Health and lots of people have relatives with mental illness."

I am simultaneously relieved that she feels so free to talk about it and embarrassed that total strangers know so much about me. I find myself wishing she had lied and told people I had appendicitis.

After visiting hours, Melinda, the recreation therapist, cons me into a game of Rummy 500. We are a diverse group along the dimensions of energy and reality testing. She tries valiantly to infuse some enthusiasm into the game, but the deck is stacked against her. We depressives outnumber any other diagnostic category and basically couldn't give a shit how the game turns out. None of us has anything better to do, so we halfheartedly play hand after hand. We forget to keep score. Rummy 500 turns into Rummy Infinity.

October 18, 1990

I awake to the news that the goddamned *Washington Post* is once again on sale at the nurses' station. We assemble around two chairs in the hall to take our turns at vital signs. Student nurses from a local college cluster together like frightened birds. We are asked if they can take our temperatures and blood pressures. I'm still sleeping badly. I feel like I've been hit by a truck and I want to tell them that, at $559 a day, no student is touching me.

But then I remember my own training. We would take in the sights like a busload of tourists, with the guide pointing out patients as particular points of interest. I recall endless case conferences in which patients were trotted out for no other purpose than our learning. In reparation, I open my mouth and stick out my arm.

The student handles me like I'm made of porcelain and has difficulty finding my pulse. Trying to diffuse her anxiety, I make a stab at a joke, suggesting that maybe I'm so depressed that I don't have one anymore. She looks alarmed and pats my shoulder, saying, "Oh, no. Don't worry. I'm sure we can find it."

She gropes around the contours of my wrist until she randomly falls upon it. She looks puzzled and protests, "But it's not where it's supposed to be."

I shrug and answer, "That's okay, neither am I." She is not amused.

I imagine her turning this interaction over in her head, dissecting it piece by piece with a clinical supervisor. Emphasis should be focused on the management of her anxiety and the handling of patients' covert hostility.

Keara bounds onto the unit, full of hugs and kisses and stories. She is almost too cheerful; her nonstop conversation seems to be her way of controlling things. She looks so tall to me tonight, especially since she is wearing my shoes. Each time she comes, she is wearing something different of mine. It breaks my heart to think of her searching through my things to find some piece of me to have and wear.

October 19, 1990

ECT number two. On the table, I close my eyes while they hook me up. Over and over, I repeat the poem fragment:

I let go of all holds then, and sank
like a hopeless swimmer into the earth . . .

No matter how many times I say it, I can't remember how it ends.

The afternoon is interminable. I ache all over and long for sleep. I feel really horrible today, deadened and anxious. I've put off taking Xanax, but I think I'll finally have to ask for some. I hate having to ask for it. It reminds me of raising your hand in grade school and having to undergo the third degree just to get permission to go to the bathroom.

The psychiatrists descend upon the unit at the same time. Men in tired suits and boring ties stride importantly up and down the halls. I conclude that Dr. Samuel is the best looking of the psychiatrists on the unit. As severely depressed as I am, it gives me comfort to know that I can still be so profoundly shallow.

The psychiatrists summon patients by loudspeaker, which has that report-to-the-principal's-office quality to it. I watch them with their expensive pens and patient charts. Like the homeless man compelled to tell the story of what he used to be before his fall, I have the urge to yell, "Hey, you guys, see me? I used to be one of you."

October 20, 1990

I slept for four straight hours last night. Dr. Samuel is delighted. He tells me that sleep is usually the first thing to improve with ECT and pronounces it a "very good sign."

Today is my seventeenth wedding anniversary and my twentieth high school reunion. Twenty years ago I was voted "Most Insightful," "Most Articulate," and "Second Most Likely to Succeed." I don't know where Miss Most-Likely-to-Succeed ended up, but my guess is that her hold on first place is still secure.

Seventeen years ago, Brian and I sat on a bed in my parents' house and, in our last-minute fashion, hastily composed our wedding vows on a small index card. Today we sit on another bed, this time in a hospital, and repeat those same words.

Every time I feel like crying, I sign myself out at the nurses' station and walk my laps around the hospital. It is a gift to feel my body in motion. Each small step walked away from the unit is an accomplishment, some small reason for joy.

October 24, 1990

Georgia, one of my favorite nurses, says that I am doing well in keeping busy, adding that it might be helpful if I give up some of my "omnipotence" about being invulnerable to the side effects of ECT. She may be right, but I refuse to give in to it. I will fight it for as long as I can and hopefully I'll know when to quit.

ECT number three. I expected that repeated exposure would desensitize me to the horror of the treatments. But they become more difficult for me over time. The hands seem rougher, the needles sharper, the band around my skull tighter, the hangover longer. Now I know how my cancer patients struggle to psyche themselves up for chemotherapy month after month. You can go through almost anything once. But to endure it each time, knowing that there will be more, and that the end is not in sight, is hard as hell.

October 25, 1990

Georgia's timing yesterday was pretty good. My memory is getting foggier. I greet my sister Priscilla like I haven't seen her in months.

"Oh Priscilla, I'm so glad to see you. I've missed you so much!"

She looks puzzled and says, "That's nice, Marth, but I was just here yesterday."

I can't remember it. Any of it. Even when she tells me what she brought and what we talked about, I can't bring it back. I have clouds in my head. I'm getting lost on the unit. I'll never admit it out loud, but when I think about going to the kitchen or the solarium, I can't really picture where they are. I

just start out walking very casually until I recognize some land-
mark that reminds me to take a left or a right. I hope no one
notices. I can't lose my walking privileges.

Dr. Samuel summons me by loudspeaker. I am struck by
two intense feelings each time I see him—surprise and nausea.
In between treatments, his features are one of the few things
that sharpen in my memory. His eyes get darker and meaner
and his teeth grow pointier. His voice lowers to a growl. And I
always remember him as very hairy. In the flesh, however, he is
a soft-spoken man with a gentle face, normal teeth, and an av-
erage amount of hair. I chalk up the distortion to a basic were-
wolf transference and the nausea to the fact that in Pavlovian
terms, he has become a powerful conditioned stimulus.

Dr. Samuel reports that the nursing staff describes me as
"easy."

"If that is true," I ask, "then why have my privileges been
downgraded from 'unaccompanied' to 'unaccompanied . . . at
nurse's discretion'?"

He answers that the nursing staff has noticed lapses in my
memory, with more confusion after each treatment. They just
want to make sure I don't go walking off and not know how to
get back. I tell him that I appreciate their concern, but that my
memory is perfectly fine and I am certainly not confused. I
can't tell whether he buys it.

"Support Group" has magically been transformed into
"Process Group." No one explains the difference, but I suspect
it has something to do with the critical mass of "high functioning" people on the unit. The group is co-led by the a nurse, who
is pretty sharp, and one of the few nurses I dislike. I'm always

surprised that people can be such tight-asses so young. She is patronizing toward us all, her voice raising in pitch and volume, each word pronounced with emphasis, like she is talking to children with auditory problems. We are each asked to articulate a goal for the session. When she turns to me I want to say, "My goal is to get through this entire session without telling you to fuck off." But then I remember my precious walking privilege and just tell her that I can't think of a goal. The sharp nurse suggests that perhaps I'd like some support from the group about my difficulties with the side effects of ECT. People in the group are dying to know more about the ECT. They ask all kinds of questions about it, and I realize that they're the first people who really want to know. My family and friends want to be reassured that it's alright. They don't really want the blow-by-blow of what actually happens. We all talk about the feeling that our lives are in shambles. It is good to know that I am not alone.

October 27, 1990

ECT number four. I am more hungover after each treatment. Even my legs ache. It's like having the flu for a day. I try to cover up the confusion as best I can, but it feels like I have the radio set between two stations. I give myself quizzes: "Where did you go on vacation last year? What was the last book you read?" And I don't know. The distant past is fine. It seems intact. But my memory for the past year is pitiful. I complain about it to a friend. He tries to reassure me. "Take it from me," he says, "you haven't missed much."

When I call home, Brian informs me that my car won't start. "It needs a jump start," he tells me, "just like its owner." I envy the simplicity of starting a weary battery. A couple of wires and the juice of an engine, all in the privacy of your own home.

I could be paranoid, but one of the older women, Marian, keeps looking at me all the time. She is about seventy-five, with a hairnet that begins in the middle of her forehead. She wears the same housedress every day, taking tiny steps in pink bedroom slippers with her stockings rolled down around her ankles. I have never seen her say a word. When I return her stare, she quickly looks away. It gives me the creeps.

When we are alone, Keara whispers shyly, "Mom, can I ask you a question about ECT?"

This is the first time she has asked any questions and I answer, "Yeah. Shoot."

"Do you spaz-out during it?"

I have no idea what she is talking about, so reflexively, I fall into my psychologist mode. When you don't have a clue what a person is saying, you just repeat the last word or two with a question mark at the end. It helps to stall for time.

"Spaz-out?" I ask.

"Yeah, you know," she says and proceeds to mime a grand mal seizure. When I tell her they give me drugs to keep my body still, she looks enormously relieved and exclaims, "Good, because I'd be so embarrassed!"

October 28, 1990

Another day at camp. Being shepherded from one stupid group to the next is my punishment for all those times my patients bitched about life on inpatient units and I told them things like "cooperate" and "get as much as you can out of it."

We in mental health sometimes assume that because we have positive intentions, our actions will automatically be positive and helpful. But benign tyranny is no less oppressive than malevolent tyranny. On psychiatric units the emphasis is on order and compliance. Patients check their autonomy at the door. The routine application of all these group and activity therapies to all people on an acute-care, high-turnover psychiatric unit is as ridiculous as prescribing the same medicine or psychotherapy to every person.

I imagine them rounding up patients on the surgical wards, insisting that all people who've just had their gallbladders removed participate in groups all day, regardless of the pain of their incisions or the drowsiness from their medications. I picture patients being required to act out their organ loss in psychodrama and fashion images of their former gallbladders in art therapy. I see them having to spill their proverbial guts in group therapy, focusing on the events in their lives that influenced their gallbladders to go bad. Whatever happened to the concept of a rest cure? Sitting in the country on a porch allowing the warmth of sunlight and the wonder of nature to convince people to go on?

One of the nurses, Diana, takes me aside and wants to talk to me about Marian, the woman who keeps staring at me. It turns out that Dr. Samuel is her doctor and he has been recommending ECT to her for some time. She is hesitant and has been watching my case with interest. Diana wonders if Marian can ask me some questions about the procedure. I tell her that it's fine with me, but remind her that no one has actually seen Marian talk, let alone ask questions.

It's lunchtime and I have rocks in my head. Everyone sits around hunched over trays of strange-colored food. Ellen's husband attempts to get her to eat, but she smacks away the food in his hand like she's batting off flies. Over and over she moans, "Oh God, please take me." Terry, with her breasts spilling out of a dress that is several sizes too small, sits down at the piano. It appears that her range extends beyond the triangle. She sings "The Impossible Dream" from *Man of La Mancha*. She doesn't sing it straight, either. She sings it like we're all in a sleazy cocktail lounge and she's taking requests at the piano bar. She belts it out, every last verse, undaunted by Ellen's divine protestations. Ellen is polite enough to synchronize her wails to coincide with those brief intervals in which Terry grabs her next breath. The rest of us sit there like zombies. We don't smile. We don't laugh. We don't even sing along. We stare at our yellowish food on pink trays like there is nothing at all unusual about this scene.

Ed gives me a bear hug so tight he lifts me off the floor. He pulls at my baggy pants and asks me if it really is better "to look good than to feel good." I assure him that it isn't and wolf down the Big Mac he's brought. It is the first food I've actually tasted and finished in months.

I can't wait for Darnell, the recreation therapist, to get here. He's great at organizing long walks that only Katherine and I go on. We walk around the neighborhood and then stop at the hospital gift shop, where Darnell buys us penny candy. He talks to me about all the "changes" he's been through in his life, especially with Vietnam and his three marriages. Sometimes he brings videos and we make popcorn and hang out watching them. My concentration is still terrible and I find it hard to follow the simplest of plots. My only consolation is that by tomorrow I won't remember anything anyway. But watching a movie seems like a normal thing to do on an empty night. And in the dark, staring at the television screen, I can almost forget where I am.

October 29, 1990

ECT number five. As much as I try to calm myself, I am always terrified in the moments before I go under. I try to slap away the oxygen mask, thinking that it is actually cutting off my air. Dr. Samuel places his hand lightly on my shoulder and says softly, "Just let yourself go to sleep now." I sink again, like a "hopeless swimmer." Reality recedes and I give in. I wake up slowly, losing my bearings, head pounding, wishing I could just stay asleep for the rest of the day. Marian must have given in to Dr. Samuel, because she is knocked out in the bed beside me.

Elaine, a lovely nurse I've met before in the recovery room, comes over to check on me. She is not her usual upbeat self. Her eyes are red and she looks so sad. I'm blitzed out of my mind from anesthesia and a grand mal seizure, but I can't help myself. I say to her in a groggy therapist voice, "You seem upset."

She bursts into tears and tells me about her mother, who is quite ill. We talk for a while about local doctors, her fears for her mother, and her uncertainty about how to help her. She holds my hand and thanks me for being so helpful to her. In the twilight zone, hooked up to all this machinery, I can't believe that I could be helpful to anyone. She asks if there is anything, anything at all, that she can do for me. I think for a moment about what I want most in this world and ask, "Can I have a Diet Coke and a chicken salad sandwich?"

I run the shower cold, trying to jolt myself back into consciousness. It is cold and rainy, so I throw on my warmest clothes, try to look really normal at the nurses' station, and sign myself out. Despite the fact that I've been walking these halls for two weeks, they now seem unfamiliar. Once I'm off the unit, I can't find the exit. The hospital is laid out with different colored arrows. I'm sure that ordinarily they are quite helpful, but they confound me now. I follow the blue arrows and then, all of a sudden, I'm following the red ones. I have no idea where I am. Confusion used to be just another word for ambivalence. At its worst it meant that I didn't understand something. But now it means that I am totally and completely lost. I start crying as I think of all the old people I've cursed in my car because they drove so slowly and didn't seem to know where the hell they were going.

Finally I recognize the gift shop where Darnell takes us for penny candy. I push my hospital bracelet higher on my wrist so that my sweater covers it and try to blend in with the other visitors. A lovely pink-haired Ladies Auxiliary volunteer asks if she can be of assistance. I want her to take me by the hand and help me find a door. I ask her to tell me where I can find a ladies' room. I pray it's not one of those "take your first left and your second right after the double doors" kinds of directions that are an obstacle to me even on a good day. Instead, she walks out of the store with me and points to a ladies' room. The bathroom door closes, slamming shut with a satisfying echo. There is a push-button lock in the knob. As bad as I feel, pressing it in gives me great satisfaction.

I splash cold water on my face. The mirror is real. My image startles me. Its clarity is painful and I long for the diffuseness of the fake mirrors on the unit. I study the woman in the glass as if she were someone else. I see the tears form in her eyes and trace a path along her nose. I see the hollowness of her cheeks, her tired hair, and the lifelessness of her face. I see her drooping shoulders and watch her throat tighten to trap the sobs that are forcing their way to daylight. I run my hands along the face in the glass as I would touch a child, and whisper, "You poor thing."

October 30, 1990

At breakfast, Marian, my ECT companion, shuffles up to me. She smiles slyly, then laughs, mumbling what sounds like "some piece of work" or "some piece of ass." I have no idea what she is talking about. But I nod and laugh along, realizing that I don't have to understand her words to share her pleasure in the recovery of her sense of humor.

Dr. Samuel and I review my case. I am sleeping five hours a night. I am eating. I am far less agitated. The weight of the depression has definitely eased. My brain feels like jelly, but he promises it won't last. He recommends that we stop with the next treatment. I can leave immediately afterward. He tells me not to drive a car for two weeks and not to return to work for several weeks. "Let yourself rest," he advises. I run down the hall to pack my bags.

October 31, 1990

ECT number six. Dr. Samuel wants to get an early start on the day. A nurse from the night staff wheels me down in darkness to the recovery room. For one last time, "I let go of all holds. . . ."

I stumble into consciousness through the heavy fog of anesthesia and the inevitable post-ECT confusion. My nurse, Sharon, bends over me and smiles. She is dressed in a long white robe. There are gold sparkles on her face. She has wings. Her head is encircled with a halo. I blink my eyes to dispel the image. But when I open them again, she is still there. Then I panic, "Oh, my God. I'm dead!"

She wheels me back to the unit where the entire staff is dressed in costume. It is impossible to shake off the clouds with nurses going about their business dressed as witches, ghosts, and clowns. I pity any poor deluded guy who gets detained today. It would probably be better for his sanity to leave him on the streets.

The ten-minute ride to our house is filled with the miracle of so many sights I never noticed in my thousands of trips down this road. I feel like Lazarus raised from the dead. Brian reaches to unlock the front door to our house. I put my hand on his and take the keys. I haven't unlocked anything in weeks, and I fumble with them. They are foreign in my hand and I forget how to differentiate the top and bottom locks. Brian and Keara set my bags on the steps and wait with tender patience. I finally find the magic key and turn it in the right direction. The lock gives way. I open the door and step back into my life again. Brian and Keara throw their arms around me. In the warmth of their embrace, my unconscious too welcomes me back. I finally remember what happens to the poor "hopeless swimmer" who kept me company during every ECT. Those elusive final lines come home to me now:

> I let go of all holds then, and sank
> like a hopeless swimmer into the earth,
> and at last came into the ease
> and the joy of that place,
> all my lost ones returning.

3

I love the dark hours of my being
in which my senses drop into the deep.
I have found in them, as in old letters,
my private life, that is already lived through,
and become wide and powerful now, like legends.
Then I know that there is room in me
for a second huge and timeless life.

Rainer Maria Rilke

October 31, 1990

My house looks exactly the same. Even the dust and clutter are like old friends welcoming me home. Still, I feel like Dorothy in *The Wizard of Oz* when she wakes up from her dream. She looks around at her familiar room and studies the faces of the people she loves. She struggles to reconcile the place she is now with the place she just left. But it's not easy. People don't understand what she's trying to say. Her body is back home in Kansas, but her head is still in Oz.

Keara comes in her nightgown and asks me to tuck her in. I am surprised because for months she has renounced being tucked in, insisting that she is too old. I am happy to oblige. Despite the long interval, we slip back into the ritual with ease. Smoothing the blankets, fluffing the pillows, putting her special comforter on top. When I lean over to kiss her good-night, she grabs my arm and whispers, "Stay a while." She scrunches over to make room for me on her high bed. I climb up and settle in next to her. "Do my eyes," she asks. I used to "do" her eyes when she was little, softly running my fingertips up and down her closed eyelids. When she was a baby, it was one of the few things that helped her fall asleep.

"Sing to me."

"What?"

"Anything but James Taylor." I stroke her eyes and sing the first song I ever sang to her—in our first night together in the hospital. It is an eighth-century Irish lullaby, "The Castle of Dromore." The words were fitting then. They fit even better now.

> October winds lament around the Castle of Dromore.
> And peace is in her lofty halls, my loving treasure's store
> Though autumn leaves may droop and die, a bud of
>   spring anew

Sing hushabye all over the land. Sing hushabye all o'er
Send no ill wind to hinder us, my helpless babe and me
Dread spirit of the black water, Clan Owen's wild banchee
And Holy Mary pity us, in heaven for grace doth soothe
Sing hushabye all over the land, sing hushabye all o'er.

Keara sleeps softly in the crook of my arm. I remain in her bed long after my mission is accomplished.

November 10, 1990

Keara is invited to spend the afternoon with her friend Natasha. Brian and I have a long list of boring but necessary errands to accomplish. Natasha runs up to the front door and invites Keara to dinner with her family. Keara is delighted, grabs her stuff, and flies out the door. I've got the list of errands, a stack of library books, and the cleaning. Brian has the newspapers for recycling and a couple of bags for the Salvation Army. We're all loaded up and ready to go. But we both hang by the door, registering the fact that we've just been handed at least eight hours alone.

"Are you thinking what I'm thinking?" Brian asks.

I dump the list, books, and clothes on the floor and answer, "I hope so."

We climb the stairs to our room and stand silent for a moment, sudden strangers who've known each other forever. Our coming together begins with the same tentative groping quality of our adolescence, but quickly turns to fluid and fire as we realize the depth of our hunger, deferred so long in these months of estrangement.

The afternoon is spent in bed. Every now and then one of us has an attack of responsibility and says, "We really should get those books back." The other one sighs and says, "Yeah, we really should," without moving an inch. We watch a video, read to each other, and eat cold Chinese food in bed—straight out of the containers.

Keara comes home at nine and finds us in our bathrobes. "What did you guys do all day?" she asks.

"Nothing much," Brian answers.

Keara shakes her head and sighs loudly. She looks at us with a mixture of pity and contempt and pronounces, "You guys are so boring."

November 15, 1990

The two weeks of driving abstinence prescribed by Dr. Samuel is technically up today. Keara needs a ride over to her friend Kate's, but Brian is not back from an errand. I tell her I can take her, grab my keys, and head for the car. We're parked on a side street. As I approach the light at the main intersection, I try to call up the file in my head that contains the directions to Keara's friends' houses. It won't come. I don't know whether to take a right or a left. I can see Kate's house in my mind. I can picture her street. But the route from here to there is nowhere.

The light changes to green. Keara is fooling with the radio and doesn't notice. A car pulls up behind us and blasts the horn.

Keara glances up and says with urgency, "Mom! Go!"

I cry out, "I don't know how to go."

The guy behind me, who has far too much testosterone in his system, pulls out and screeches around me, flashing me a look of disdain and saluting me with his middle finger. My mind is jammed. My body is paralyzed. Feeling totally humiliated, my first impulse is to turn around and go home.

Keara says, "Don't worry, Mom. That guy was a real ass-hole."

"Keara," I ask sanctimoniously, "do you kiss your mother with that mouth?"

She laughs and retorts, "Oh, like you should talk." I laugh back.

"I can get us there, Mom. If you just do it once, I bet it will all come back to you."

So I drive and she navigates. Keara is no Vasco da Gama in the directions department either, which makes for an interesting ride. We pull up to Kate's about twenty minutes late, but there nonetheless.

"Are you gonna be okay getting home, Mom?" Keara asks with concern.

"Yeah, babe, I'll be fine," I assure her. I make a number of wrong turns and tour parts of the county I've never seen before. But I try to stop worrying and let my memory unfold as I go, allowing instinct to replace conscious thought. It works, even though it means taking the long way home.

November 20, 1990

My first session with Kay since the hospital. She greets me at the door with a wide smile and open arms. I fill her in on the hospital, the ECT, the vast improvement in how I'm feeling and doing. She is delighted with the progress, but warns me that the process of recovery from a depression as severe as mine is not a smooth ascending slope. It is instead a "saw-toothed" profile, with numerous peaks and valleys. She tells me that people coming out of bad depressions often panic when they hit a decline, but that it is all part of the pattern of recovery. This is not news I want to hear. I want the smooth ascending slope. If I get the peaks and valleys, I'll deal with them when it happens.

I bitch to her about the hospital, about my life being in shreds, about feeling like a stranger in familiar territory. She encourages me to articulate any of the good things that have come from the experience. I refuse to consider the fact that this cloud had anything approaching a silver lining. She seizes on the fact that I finally stopped pretending to be fine when I wasn't. I let people help me, really take care of me. She's right. It is especially true with my family, in its bringing me closer to my parents, from whom I've always asserted such strong independence. It is clear in the role reversals with my brothers and sisters. No longer am I the oldest child who has everything under control. It was strange to be vulnerable with Mark and Rachel, the "little kids" of the family. But after the initial hesitance, it felt pretty good.

November 21, 1990

Ed and Ginger had a baby boy yesterday. Ed calls tonight.

"Marth, can you do me a favor?"

A favor? No one has asked me for a favor in months.

"Sure," I answer tentatively. "What do you need?"

"Ginger and Conor are being discharged tomorrow morning. I'll have Maddie with me and I have a feeling it's going to be a zoo trying to get everything together and keep Maddie entertained at the same time. Can you come and help smooth the transition?"

I try to figure out how many people he's called before me, since mine is not the first name that would occur, even to me, when the subject of "smoothing transitions" arises. I ask if he wouldn't rather have Brian.

"Well, we were really hoping for you," he answers.

"What time do you want me?" I ask him, choking back tears.

Sometimes being asked for a favor is such a burden. At other times it is such a gift.

November 22, 1990

I do not look forward to going to my parents' for Thanksgiving. This year has been hard for almost every member of my family—the dissolution of a marriage and an engagement, depression, addiction, life-threatening illness, accidents, and the estrangement of one family member. Not exactly a banner year. I am afraid that coming together will only multiply the pain and magnify our losses. And if just coming together isn't enough, the prospect of giving thanks for it all seems overwhelming.

Surprisingly, with the exception of my sister Sarah, everyone shows. The hors d'oeuvre course goes easily enough. We engage in witty banter and small talk until my mother summons us to find our assigned seats around the long table. As is the custom, my father makes the sign of the cross, bows his head, and begins to say grace. He's alright while he stays in the "Bless us, O Lord, for these thy gifts . . . " part of the praying. It's when he ventures into the free-form extemporaneous portion of the program that all the trouble begins. He intones, "Lord, we thank you for the many ways in which you have blessed our family this year. . . ." As he's praying, I look across the table and see that my sister Rachel's shoulders are shaking. Her head is bowed. Her eyes are closed. She is clearly fighting to maintain control, so I assume she's holding back tears. She explodes with laughter. It's one of those fits of laughter that is partly funny, but mostly anxious.

My father, who has forty years of uninterrupted prayer-leading under his belt, looks dumbfounded and stops praying. She blurts out, "Dad, I'm sorry, but what are you talking about? This is the worst year this family has ever had!" Everyone chimes in, roundly criticizing his prayer and reinforcing Rachel's perception that this has definitely not been a year of blessings.

My mother tolerates the general grousing for several minutes and then tries to get us back on track, saying, "Well, at least we're all together." There is a collective, if grudging sigh of endorsement. We fold our hands, bow our heads, and wait for the prayer to resume. My father inhales deeply and opens his mouth to take another shot at grace. Simultaneously, my brother Chip registers the obvious fact that Sarah is missing and challenges my mother's wish to offer thanks for the intactness of our family. "Wait a minute," he complains, "we can't pray about that. We're not all together."

My father is once again silent and bewildered. His six years in the seminary never prepared him for handling challenges to prayers.

We laugh self-consciously, acknowledging the pain of the estrangement and the futility of our attempts to deny it. Priscilla makes a motion to abandon grace altogether and move on to the eating portion of the meal. The motion is heartily seconded. My parents protest and with whatever authority they can muster in the face of such mutiny, they forbid anyone to touch a crumb of food until the prayer is finished.

By now, the steam has evaporated over the platters and bowls of food. We engage in a major debate, with each person expressing his or her own unique qualms about praying. The underlying theme, however, is basically the same: How can we possibly bless this bread when we feel so bad?

My brother Mark, a drummer in a heavy-metal rock band, complete with shoulder-length hair, earring, tattoo, and black leather pants, is noticeably quiet during this whole process. As he's the person who's probably logged the least amount of time within a church, I figure he must be frustrated with all this praying nonsense. He pounds his fist against the table and instantly commands everyone's attention.

"Damn it," he protests, "I'm thankful. I'm thankful that I survived this year. And I thank God that you all did too."

My brother-in-law Darrell, who at the tender age of forty is recovering from vascular surgery, responds with a resounding "Amen!"

We sit in silence for several moments, each of us absorbing my brother's words and applying them to our own situations. One by one, we offer our personal assent to his declaration. Chip yields the floor to my father, saying, "Take it, Dad. . . ."

For the third time, my father bows his head, inhales cautiously, and prays, "God, we give you thanks that we survived this year. We pray for those who didn't and we ask for the strength to survive another year." We answer with a unanimous and enthusiastic chorus of amens.

The food, by this point, is stone cold. But no one moves. We just look at each other, holding on to this moment, this connection, this prayer-by-consensus.

"Will someone please pass the potatoes?" demands Rachel, reminding us of the feast before us. I help myself to the cranberries and smile, remembering all the foolish times when I've groped around blindly for what I needed, never realizing that the sustenance I craved was right at hand.

November 28, 1990

On the phone with Pat I say, "I just started a really interesting book, *The Passion* by Jeanette Winterson."

There is a long pause on the other end of the line. "Martha," Pat tells me hesitantly, "you already read that book."

Another humble moment followed by a brief silence.

"Well," I try to recover, "did I like it?"

I can almost hear Pat smile on the other end. "Oh, yeah," she says, "keep reading. You loved it!"

December 3, 1990

I see Elaine, the first patient scheduled since I've been out of the hospital. I am nervous that I've forgotten her life, in the same way that I've forgotten the way to Keara's friends' houses. She sits down across from me and after a brief "How are you feeling?" picks up right where we left off. As soon as I see her, everything comes back. Her life, her pain, the names of her dogs and her neighbors.

She feels lousy, struggling with a depression, not as severe as mine but weighing down on her heavily and making each hour a challenge. For a moment I panic, thinking that I don't know how to help people anymore.

But I summon the images of Lew and Kay, and Jeremy before them. I remind myself that the essence of hell for me was its finality, its inescapability. Going in to see them week after week, awkward and mute and hopeless, was evidence of my fight against the finality. Each time I entered their offices I gave silent testimony to the possibility of breaking out of hell. Despite the dead ends and infuriatingly blind alleys, despite the frustration and embarrassment, despite every awful drug side effect, having a companion on the journey helps. It is so easy for me to forget the importance of the companionship itself when things aren't going well for my patients. I tend to look only at actual outcomes to judge my goodness as "doctor." But my memories of my own doctors remind me that the process of just walking the road with someone is so important. The communication of hope, the administration of gentleness, and the sharing of some part of self can make a long lonely journey, in all its circuitousness, almost bearable.

So I walk along the road with Elaine for the hour, still uncertain of the path, but familiar with the terrain.

December 18, 1990

Reliable people stand me up for appointments. When I call to check, they say they "forgot," which in therapy language often means "I'm mad at you."

I have referred twelve-year-old Stacy to a neurologist for a consultation regarding her sleep problems. Her appointment is scheduled for the end of the week. When I bring it up in our session, Stacy wonders aloud what this new doctor will look like. I encourage her to verbalize what she imagines. She gives a vivid description of her fantasy about the new doctor.

"I love to guess about people I haven't met yet," she tells me. "But I'm always wrong."

"How?" I ask.

"Well, like with you, I thought you would be young . . . and thin."

The phone rings during dinner. Keara flies to it and returns breathlessly to the table, asking for permission to go shopping with a friend.

"It's a school night," I tell her. "Absolutely not."

"But Mom," she protests.

"No!" I insist.

She yells at me, "I thought you, of all people, would understand!" She slams the kitchen door and the phone, stomps up the stairs, and slams her bedroom door.

I look over at Brian, who seems to be enjoying himself. "Why is everybody so pissed at me all of a sudden?" I ask.

He smiles, "Because, Marth, now they know that you can take it."

He's right. It's a case of the good news and the bad news. The good news is that I'm "back in business." The bad news is that every now and then, someone is going to think that I'm a real asshole.

December 24, 1990

Patricia, Patrick, and kids come for our annual Christmas Eve dinner. Brian and I compute that it is the first time in over a year that we've had anyone over for dinner and declare it a sure index of improvement. Our two families squeeze around the table. Keara and Mara light the Advent wreath and our faces glow in the light of the pink and purple candles. David and Suzanne take great pleasure in dipping an evergreen branch in water and sprinkling us with a blessing. Brian reads from Paul's letter to the Romans (13:12):

> The night is advanced,
> the day is at hand. Let us then
> throw off the works of darkness
> and put on the armor of light.

With that we dig into dinner and then delight in the exchange of gifts.

After everyone has gone, Brian, Keara, and I do a cursory cleaning of the kitchen and gather in the living room. Keara lights the many tiny candles around the room. Brian encourages the waning fire. As is our custom, Keara opens one gift from us. Then we open hers. Bursting with pride, she presents us with books that she bought and had gift wrapped at Brentano's. On my card she has written, "I love you, Mommy. This is the best present I've ever gotten you." It is a book of poetry by Wendell Berry.

To know your child in all her moods and changes is one kind of gift. To have your child know you is quite another. When she tunes into me, picks up on a phrase or a feeling, even with her wicked mimicry, there is an utter sense of resonance. It is the knowledge that this separate being, who began as a part of me, is still a part of me. We have that knowledge of each other deep within us. She knew that book would give me pleasure. It does. It always will.

January 1, 1991

Emerging from a long depression seems to happen on two levels—one almost in an instant, in the moment that something clicks on, like heat switching on in the middle of a cold night. The other happens incrementally–when you feel yourself actually making progress, inching up, out of, and away from that deep darkness that was home for much too long. The first level is so quick. The second level takes too damn long.

January 5, 1991

I have been reading and consulting with people on the issue of how long I will need to continue antidepressant medication. There is consistent agreement that I am probably looking at a lifetime of antidepressants or, as some people have recommended, mood stabilizers such as lithium. I keep trying to label my experiences with depression as *episodes,* but they keep using words like *chronic, recurrent,* and *cyclic.* I hate their words. I want my depression to be over, totally and completely over.

The most painful part of this is the decision about trying for another baby. Everyone has a different opinion. I've talked with experts who recommend against pregnancy. There are people who support the continuation of medicine in a carefully monitored pregnancy. There are people who suggest that if I go off medicine to get pregnant and become seriously depressed again, that ECT could be used again with low risk to the baby. The alternatives they propose are equally awful. I couldn't bear it if I was responsible for harming a baby. As much as Brian longs for another child, he agrees that the stakes are too high for even a calculated risk. The depression may be over, but I am still paying the price.

The bottom line is that I don't have any more miscarriages in me. I don't have the courage or the strength to take any more risks, and I can't tolerate the next few years of constant ambivalence. I am going to talk to Rob about a tubal ligation. I'm just going to try to be grateful for what I've got.

January 9, 1991

I talk with Kay about my anxiety at picking up the shambles of my life—my family, friendships, work, even play. I talk about my decision about the tubal ligation. Nothing in my life was spared by this natural disaster, this "act of God."

I confess to her that my spiritual life is in the toilet. I don't believe in anything anymore except luck—good and bad. I still feel like I'm being punished for being a bad person, a weak person, a neurotic person. It is hard to reconcile my old concept of a merciful God with my recent experience of a hateful, spiteful God, or a totally indifferent God who plays fifty-two-pickup with people's lives. What did I do to deserve what I got? Will God keep me permanently on the shit list? Will I ever be forgiven?

Kay listens to my rantings and smiles. "Martha," she says, "I don't think we're talking about God forgiving *you*. I think we're talking about you forgiving *God*."

January 15, 1991

Brian, Keara, and I watch a show about a pregnant woman. In one scene, she has a sonogram. The doctor points out the baby's head and its feet. The woman is ecstatic when she sees her child's beating heart. What I see on the screen and what is burned in my memory are identical, with one exception. My baby's heart stopped beating. A crushing pain hits like lightning and I start to cry before I even know I'm sad. Brian stiffens and looks like he wishes I would leave the room. Keara puts a hand on my shoulder.

"I'm okay," I tell Brian, in the middle of heaving sobs.

"No," he yells, "you're not okay!"

I yell back, "I'm just sad, alright? Aren't I allowed to be sad?" And then I throw in the zinger, "Besides, you weren't even there." I fly out of the room and down the stairs.

I sit on the living room couch and cry my eyes out. It is so hard for Brian to understand the difference between grief and depression. He becomes frightened whenever he sees me in pain. But this pain isn't depression. It is sorrow at something I've lost. It will never go away. This loss is part of me. In some ways, I don't want to lose it. It has receded as a major presence in my life, but every now and then it comes out, demanding a bit of memory and attention. And I always feel better after I give it a little of what it wants.

Keara tiptoes downstairs, puts her arms around me, and asks, "Aren't I enough?" I tell her that she is more than enough, and try to explain that sometimes sadness comes calling anyway. We talk for a while. She says, "I think God made things this way because I'm probably going to turn out to be something great and it wouldn't be fair for a brother or a sister to have to live up to that." I smile and tell her that I'm really concerned about her low self-esteem. She tells me that she is afraid because her life, so far, has been good and easy. She is frightened that something bad might happen that will forever change the course of her life. I remind her that she's already been through a number of difficult things and handled them well. She shakes her head and says wistfully, "No, Mom. They don't count."

Brian joins us downstairs. He puts his arm around me and whispers, "Sorry, I just get scared when I see you upset." I tell him that he has to understand that no amount of "mental health" is going to take away the sorrow of loss. He laughs self-consciously and replies, "Maybe we need some kind of a code to help me know the difference."

January 23, 1991

I tell Kay about my sense that the actual depression is gone, but many of the painful feelings persist. She likens it to post-traumatic stress, where the need is often to repeat the stories over and over, filling in the holes and gaps of the past two years and integrating them with my current life. I tell her the pain keeps coming back in flashes of new feelings, new memories. It comes bearing bruises that I think are so old that they can't possibly hurt. But then I bump up against them and the pain is immediate and severe.

I am noticing, though, that each time they come, they hurt a bit less and I win a bit of distance. Each time the camera pans out a bit farther. I begin to see the big picture, rather than every minuscule and excruciating detail.

February 4, 1991

My tubal ligation is scheduled for the sixteenth. I see it marked on the calendar, squeezed right in there among the meetings, dinners, and haircut appointments. I feel a tentative sense of resolution about this, but it doesn't stop the sadness. My friends who have had tubal ligations know exactly what I mean. They admit that it's a chapter that is painfully hard to end. On the brighter side, they encourage me to imagine life without a diaphragm and remind me of the pleasures of sex without birth control.

We hit the neighborhood Italian restaurant for dinner and discuss the arrangements for the sixteenth over coffee. Keara, who is clearly paying attention in her sex education classes, playfully yanks Brian's chain about a tubal ligation versus a vasectomy.

"Don't you think Mom's done enough in the childbearing department?" she teases. "Why don't you do your part?"

Brian blanches. In keeping with the custom of the restaurant, the waitress brings the fresh fruit of the day, which happens to be bananas. I take one, peel it, and cavalierly slice a piece off.

"Yeah, Brian," I say. "See, nothin' to it."

He looks like he's going to choke and complains, "Have you noticed lately that everything is the girls against the boy?"

Keara, who is thoroughly enjoying herself, says, "Yeah, Dad. And you better get used to it."

February 14, 1991

I go to the hospital for my presurgery registration. The woman at the desk takes more information than could possibly be relevant, but I spit it out like a computer. Then comes the hard part.

"Number of pregnancies?"

"Three."

"Number of live births?"

"One."

"Is the child still living?"

"Yes, very much."

"So you have just the one child?"

"Yes. Just the one."

As I say the words, a door slams shut in my mind. One and always one.

The woman asks casually, "So, you gonna take the rest of the week off?"

I give her a puzzled look and reply, "No, my doctor told me I can go back to work the next day."

She hoots loudly, leans over, and slaps my hand, "Girlfriend, your doctor's a man, right?"

I nod. "Yes."

"Honey, only a man would say a damn-fool thing like that. Do yourself a favor. Take the week off. You're gonna need it."

I smile at her politely, but inside I resolve that everything is in place and will go exactly as planned. I even have a racquetball court reserved in two days.

February 16, 1991

The surgery goes exactly as expected. In a burst of female machismo and a narcotic high, I smugly congratulate myself that the registration woman was wrong. I should know by now that thoughts like these are always, for me, the kiss of death. I inhale two Cokes in the recovery room and then two sugar cookies that Keara and I made last week.

I develop a nasty allergic reaction to either the anesthesia or the pain medication, and God, do I pay for those Cokes and those cookies. I vomit continuously for almost sixteen hours. With each wave of nausea I am flooded by the revolting smell of vanilla and visions of those little gingerbread men, valentine hearts, and pointy stars dancing around in my stomach, preparing for a return trip up my esophagus. I'm sure that the violence of the headache will kill me, and after about ten hours, I hope it does. At times like these, it is impossible to remember when I ever felt well or to imagine that I ever will again.

I pull myself out of bed, throw on the clothes that are lying at the bottom of my closet, and head for the grocery store. The place is packed, with people brandishing long lists and wielding their shopping carts like weapons. I am weak and wasted, but the siege in my stomach has ended and the sledge-hammer in my head has quieted.

Rounding the corner of aisle fourteen, I find that it is mercifully almost empty. I park the cart and search for Brian's brand of tea. I never realized before that there are so many kinds of tea. There are, of course, the basic and boring generic teas. But the rest of the section is crammed with an array of infinite possibilities. There are comforting titles like Sweet Dreams and Sleepy Time and zesty little numbers like Wild Berry Zinger and Apricot Delight. I am utterly captivated by the colors of the boxes and the sweet exotic scents that permeate the plastic wrapping—cinnamon, chamomile, passion-flower, jasmine, orange blossom—sights and smells I have never noticed in my hundreds of trips down this aisle.

I can't get over the wonder of it all. Twenty-four hours ago I was glued to my bathroom floor and now here I am—vertical in the tea aisle. A little banged up, but essentially intact, delighting in the magnificence of tea. I am overflowing with so much happiness that I have enough to share with my down-trodden fellow shoppers. There is only one other person in the aisle. She is bent over cans of evaporated milk, frowning and performing price comparisons on a tiny calculator. Her dour expression stops me in my tracks. Sometimes bliss is best kept to oneself.

I realize that in the past forty-eight hours I've done one of those quick tours of the circuit from birth to death and just come out on the other side to resurrection. Epiphanies like these are so much more likely to occur for me in grocery stores and laundromats, rather than in the more traditional places of reverence and prayer. They are moments in which the baseline about what is good and important in my life changes. Often they come just when it feels like life has played another rotten trick on me and nothing in my life is ever going to go as I expect. Through these hardships comes the realization that it is in the most ordinary aspects of my life—the ones in which everything can, and does, go wrong—that I am offered glimpses of the extraordinary. In these flashes of insight, I understand for a moment that one of the great dividends of darkness is an increased sensitivity to the light. And in these rare and expansive moments, I am called to delight. Even if it's only in tea.

February 24, 1991

My friend Jennifer invites me to a women's ritual in celebration of Candlemas. Women's ritual. I wish there were a better way of saying that. "Women's ritual" sounds like it involves sacrificing virgins or drinking menstrual blood. I am alternately drawn to and repelled by these women's spiritual things. I am hungry for some sort of religious experience that will fit for me. At the same time, many of these attempts seem so contrived.

Candlemas has ancient traditions in marking the halfway point between the winter solstice and the beginning of spring.

We are told to wear white and bring food. I throw on a white turtleneck over a pair of jeans.

When I arrive, I see that the women are dressed totally in white. The only place you'll see more white is at a first communion or a Klan rally. We drink club soda from champagne glasses until everyone arrives and then we gather in the living room where a pastel-colored sheet, dotted with votive candles, is spread out on the floor.

Susan introduces the evening and reads several lovely pieces. We go around the circle introducing ourselves, invoking the spirits of our foremothers. "I am Martha, daughter of Mary Louise, granddaughter of Mildred and Frances . . . and I celebrate the goddess within." We dip our hands in a bowl of water and bless the goddess to our right. Susan asks us to say something about marriage for a woman who is getting married for the second time. It starts out beautifully and then slowly gets weird when a couple of women start crying about the rottenness of their own relationships, which is not quite the prenuptial send-off that was intended.

A woman to my left bursts into song. It's not a song that everyone knows so that we can sing along. She just makes it up as she goes. This tops out at the weirdness level for me and I feel uncontrollable laughter rising up in me. At first it has the intensity of a giggle, but builds in strength until it becomes a downright guffaw. I know that there will be little tolerance in this group for my own personal brand of spontaneity. Women at these events take themselves incredibly seriously. In order to keep from laughing out loud, I have to resort to a desperate trick from my childhood.

It comes from all those days when we were herded into church and made to kneel down, backs straight, hands folded, fingers pointing toward heaven. We would recite the rosary or the stations of the cross, droning on and on with the repetition of prayers. Things would happen during those times that would not be particularly funny in a different context, but were hysterical just because we were in church—the last place on earth you were supposed to find amusement.

To control the laughter, I pictured the consequences: punishment and humiliation from an angry nun, ranging from the verbal, "So you think Christ's suffering is funny, do you? Christ who bled and died on the cross for your sins!" to the physical, getting my hair pulled or having to kneel for the rest of the afternoon. Nothing worked. The only thing that helped was the macabre imagery of picking out a member of my family and thinking about that person dead. Not dead in the abstract. Dead in the casket. I pictured the scene as realistically as possible, focusing on my total devastation at the loss. On really funny days, I'd start with my parents and end up burying the whole family. I resort to this old trick now, at this weird event. Luckily, it still works.

We bless our chakras, dipping our hands in water and reciting the blessing aloud as we progress through the different body parts. As I reach down, sprinkle water, and repeat, "I bless my vagina . . . ," I picture all the maternal ancestors I invoked earlier in the evening giving a slow groan and turning over in their graves.

We share our wishes for the coming spring. I talk about this winter as a time of sterility for me, literally and figuratively, and express my frustration at not being able to break out of it. Susan talks about the progression of winter to spring. She says that there is a need for winter, for seeds to be dormant in the darkness, for change to be anticipated but not yet realized. She warns that I can push and push, but like a seed in the ground, some things just aren't going to emerge until they're good and ready.

Susan puts on some African tribal drum music. We choose noisemakers and dance around her dining room. The image of a bunch of white women in white clothes trying to dance like Africans is hysterical to me. The dance is interminable, but at least I don't have to bury my family. My outright laughter just looks like I'm having one hell of a good time.

It's safe to say that I am going to have to continue my search for a spiritual home.

March 6, 1991

We spend the evening at Ed and Ginger's. The place is literally crawling with babies. I can't get away from nursing mothers, adorable infants, and combative toddlers. Children dominate the scene, with each couple trying to strike a tentative balance about whose turn it is to do what for whom. Everyone has his or her hands full, except for Brian and me. Keara stays for the first hour and plays easily with the children. Her friends Natasha and Kate drop by to pick her up and she departs for her own evening plans. When the door closes behind her, our harried friends make envious remarks about our freedom.

In the midst of these babies, with Keara off to her own world, I am sideswiped by the most terrific pain. A sadness sweeps through and almost knocks the air out of me. I can point to the place where it hurts. My chest is heavy. My breathing becomes sighing. My eyes fill up, my throat constricts, and

I maintain a frozen smile while my mind says to the rest of me, "For God's sake, stay in control. This will pass." And it does.

I bend over and pick up the baby who is licking my shoe. She burrows into me and I bury my face in her neck, relishing her delicious infant smell. There is a certain sweetness to this sort of sorrow. It has a source and a destination. It is finite. I can locate it and name it. The sweetness is in the knowing. There is great comfort in that.

I lift the baby high in the air and swing her back and forth. She giggles and gurgles in contagious delight. In the presence of such a treasure, there is nothing else for me to do but accept it. I swing her up high again and giggle and gurgle right back.

March 15, 1991

Telling people I've had ECT is a real conversation killer. People seem to be more forthright these days about discussing depression. Things have loosened up, even talking about medicine. Hell, the cashier in the grocery store told me yesterday that she's on Prozac. But ECT is in a different class. For months, in my conversations with most people, I have glossed over ECT's contribution to the end of my depression. But lately I've been thinking, "Damn it. I didn't rob a bank. I didn't kill anybody. I have nothing to be ashamed of." I've started telling people about the ECT. My admission is typically met with uncomfortable silences and abrupt shifts in topics.

An acquaintance at a party is outraged. "How could you let them do that to you?"

I bristle and answer, "I didn't let them do it to me. I asked them to do it."

"But why would you ever do that?" she insists.

"Because I was trying to save my life," I answer, hoping this will end the conversation.

Emboldened by a couple of bourbons, she challenges, "Aren't you being just a bit dramatic? Depression is hardly a life-and-death condition."

"You want to bet?" I answer. "I was as close to death as I ever want to get."

"Well, it's your life, I guess."

"Yes, you bitch," I think. "It is my life and what right do you have to judge me?" In the interests of sociability, I keep my mouth shut and wander off to a cluster of people I recognize.

I fume all evening. Damn her. Damn all of them. Nobody bats an eye when electricity is delivered to a stalled heart. There is no outcry. In fact, it's considered a miracle. A person passes from life to death to life again through the application of electric current to the heart. But try talking about the same thing with the brain, and it's no miracle. Suddenly, words like *torture* and *mind control* populate the descriptions.

I'm not about to stand on street corners urging people to try electroconvulsive treatment. I will never be the ECT poster-girl. I am the first to admit the downside—confusion and memory loss. But damn it, it worked. I didn't want to have it. Who would? I didn't want to have a caesarean section either. I ended up with a terrible infection, a long scar, and a difficult recovery. But I got Keara. A beautiful healthy new life. It was no picnic. But I'd do it again in a heartbeat.

April 2, 1991

After a morning of errands, I come home to find a bunch of tulips stuck in our mail slot. They are wrapped in paper towels and a plastic grocery bag without a note. These are not the usual tulips. They are huge, with large stalks and petals as big as the curved palm of my hand. I gather them in my best vase and install them on the hall table. They are breathtaking—a fiery red-orange opening to reveal the most incredible golden stars in their centers. Each time I catch sight of them, I am enthralled. I lose my focus, my balance. No matter what I'm doing, I have to stop and go over to peek inside to assure myself that the gold stars are still there. They always are, and for a moment I let myself believe in God again.

April 4, 1991

In a true role reversal, I pontificate to Brian, who is anxious about money, that if we have our health nothing else matters. The ability to breathe and to be is such a tremendous gift that anything lacking in our lives is cheap in comparison.

Each time I pass the hall table with the tulips I have to catch my breath. They open slowly, seductively, changing over the days in color and shape. I am sorry to know that the more they open, the closer they are to their demise. But their opening is so magnificent that it is easy to forget about their inevitable end. Before they die, they open out so far that they look like children's pinwheels. One strong breath will blow them apart. I tiptoe around them and mourn each petal that can no longer suspend itself in the air and has to let go.

April 11, 1991

In between sessions I dash across the street to grab a late, quick, and nutritious lunch from 7-Eleven. I wolf down a hot dog and dispense myself the biggest of the Big Gulps. The junior high school is just letting out as I head back to the office. People waiting to cross the street gather on the corner. A young black girl in a canary yellow jumpsuit dances in defiance of the DO NOT WALK sign above our heads. She is infused with the sunlight that melts her bones and makes her golden. She is plugged into a Walkman and moves to her own private music, the rhythm known only to her. Pale people trudge by. A car stalls in traffic, and I think how long this winter has been and what I would give to be that loose and golden. I wonder about the laws of osmosis and how many rules I would break to move like her. But the light changes. And as I walk stiffly back to work, she savors the first morsels of spring.

May 7, 1991

Today is sizzling hot, the sun so consistently strong that even with all our obsessive SPF protection, we show it. From the golden honey brown on my niece Chelsea to the fire-engine-red "Irish suntan" on Priscilla, we have shed our pale winter skins. It is so easy to be still in the sunlight. I feel my weight against the plastic lounge chair as I begin to settle like the contents of a package.

My neck goofs off and lets my head find its own means of support. My back melts into the strips of plastic and beach towel. My butt goes flat (as flat as my butt ever gets) and soft. My legs lengthen and fall apart, with my feet flopping around almost independent of my will. The sun melts out the alertness in me, the readiness to spring into action. I should be swimming laps . . . but I don't care. I should be writing . . . but I don't care. Well, goddamn it, at the very least, I should be reading . . . but I don't care.

These oases of time in which I am simultaneously loose and awake are rare for me and I'm beginning to learn to protect them when they occur. The realization that these moments have value in themselves is still a difficult concept for me to grasp, since the only way I've ever known or liked myself has been in motion.

May 24, 1991

In the midst of discussing cases with several colleagues, someone refers to a patient as "a thirty-five-year-old manic-depressive." I cringe, mentally leave the case discussion, and retreat into my own head. My reaction to the common "shorthand" for describing patients is puzzling to me.

I think about the difference between *having* something and *being* something. They are only words, but I'm struck by how much they convey about the manner in which the shorthand of mental illness reduces the essence of people in ways that labels for other serious illnesses do not.

People say, "I have cancer." They don't say, "I am cancer." People say, "I have heart disease," not "I am heart disease." Somehow the presumption of a person's individuality is not compromised by those diagnostic labels. All the labels tell us is that the person has a specific challenge with which he or she struggles in a highly diverse life. But call someone "a schizophrenic" or "a borderline" and the shorthand has a way of closing the chapter on the person. It reduces a multifaceted human being to a diagnosis and lulls us into a false sense that those words tell us who the person is, rather than only telling us how the person suffers.

June 15, 1991

Somewhere, somehow, I've lost the gift of being. It comes to me slowly as I notice that I'm crossing into familiar and awful territory. At first I chalk it up to a bad day, too much work, or the many excuses I can muster to make the fall seem logical and linear in cause and effect. But then it spills into the next day and the next. Time slows down. I lose my sense of place. It's like I've been walking along a flat surface with the horizon stretching out effortlessly in front of me. But then comes the incline, the slope growing steeper with time. All of a sudden I don't know the where or the why of my destination. All I know is that I just have to keep on walking.

My first impulse when I feel like this is to withdraw from people, so they won't see me as an emotional cripple and write me off. But the people closest to me make that very difficult. I am blessed with such kindness from my family, my friends, my doctors.

Ed grabs me in the hall in the few seconds we have between patients.

"Do you feel as shitty as you look?"

I nod.

He throws a quick arm around me and quotes a line we've always loved from *The Hotel New Hampshire*, "Keep passing the open windows."

It's only a second. It's only a sentence. But I feel known right down to my bones.

Lew arranges for me to have a test to determine the level of medicine in my blood. He calls with the results. The levels have plummeted. He increases the dosage. The good news is that we know the cause of this depression. The bad news is that this has happened before and we don't know what keeps causing the levels to drop.

June 18, 1991

A woman comes to me for consultation, referred by her oncologist because she is depressed. She fumes at me for giving such lousy directions and makes it clear that seeing me is not her idea and that she has no intention of returning. Sometimes, in situations like these, I have the good sense to keep my mouth shut long enough for people to tell me their real stories. In the silence, her anger gives way quickly to tears. She tells me about her mastectomy and the recurrence of her breast cancer. The cancer is eating her up from the inside out, resulting in ulcerations all over her chest. She wrestles with words that could possibly convey her suffering. As she tries to talk to me, deep wrenching sobs drown out the words. Her cries come from that place in us where hell resides. Where we find ourselves in total darkness, alone and afraid. Each time she tries to attach some bit of language to her experience, she becomes more frustrated and drifts farther and farther away.

"Sometimes," I admit to her, "hell has no words."

Her sobbing quiets. Her breathing deepens. She looks straight at me and begins to unbutton her blouse. I want to stop her and say, "Oh, no. I'm not that kind of doctor." But I realize she knows that already. She unbuttons her blouse and holds it open. She is wearing nothing underneath. What she shows me has no words. Her skin is ravaged with scars and huge sores, conjuring up childhood images of Job, with Satan "smiting him with boils." Looking at her, I remember the lepers that the nuns used to tell us about, leaving little to a young girl's imagination. Never have I seen anything so horrible, so painful.

She holds her blouse open and looks me in the eye with a mixture of pain and defiance. The pain is in the tears that trace their way along her face. The defiance is in her jaw, the curve of her mouth, the stiffening of her neck. She defies me. To what? Flinch? Turn away? Feel pity? Say something totally inept? I don't know. All I know is that I need to stare her right back in the eye and stop fighting so hard to keep my own eyes from filling up.

She tells me that she can't even show her husband and daughter the ravages of her cancer. In acknowledging the torment of her isolation, I understand what I have to do with her for the rest of this hour. I have to sit with her, with her blouse open, and her awful wounds, both visceral and psychic. I have to sit with her in her pain.

The quiet between us is punctuated by brief exchanges about her life. But it is clear that she doesn't really want my words. She wants my presence.

When the hour is up, she buttons her blouse. She straightens herself up, thanks me, and shakes my hand. She tells me that she doesn't think she'll be back and adds, "I wish you were a priest." I tell her that sometimes I wish that too. She says good-bye and leaves the way she came, bitching about my directions.

Grateful that my next hour is free, I sink back into my chair to absorb what just happened. I wonder what more I could have said or done with her, and I pray that she finds her priest. That woman reminds me, again, of what it means to be a therapist. It means sitting there and looking squarely at people's pain. It means watching as they peel back layer after layer, knowing that as they go deeper, it gets more painful for them, and for you. It means being with them even when all those wonderful turns of language we learned in our training turn to dust and blow away. It means acknowledging that sometimes hell, indeed, has no words. You just have to take the tour. Sometimes it's all you can do to look them straight in the eye without flinching. You have to learn what to say and you have to learn how to shut up. And sometimes it's enough.

July 3, 1991

Each time the darkness comes I try to remind myself that it will not last. It will hurt me, but it won't kill me. We know why this is happening. I just have to wait it out until the stronger dose of medicine kicks in.

All the romantic nonsense about depression somehow making one into a creature of unique sensibilities is easy to agree with when I feel good. Then I'm sharper, superior for having weathered something terribly difficult, or just plain pleased at having narrowly gotten away with something once again—like the snow day after the night's homework I didn't do. All of it stands up to the light, but it's bullshit in the shadows. I don't care about unique sensibilities. All I care about is surviving. My goal in life is just to get through the days.

I pull myself together and take a walk down the park road, along the winding paths of red sand packed with gravel. There is a light breeze and the plentiful Queen Anne's lace dances with it. Not all orderly, like "everyone sway this way." No, they're all mixed up in each other—dancing in a tangle of green and white that makes me smile, remembering damp gymnasiums filled with tall girls and lesser-developed boys. We always found a way to let our bodies touch—at least as much as any nun would allow—and still keep approximate time to the music.

The greater pleasures are farther ahead. I climb the slope of the dunes and see the sun over the island and the water. The sky is streaked pink and purple and yellow. There is a dark out-line of children playing in the distance. I find a bench. Two boys play catch in front of me and critique each other's throws. Couples climb the dunes. Men try to capture the moment on video. The sun is huge in its departure, commanding everyone's reverent attention. I watch as it leaves the horizon and follow its descent without moving, without blinking.

Once more, I acknowledge the possibility of God. In my own narcissistic and grandiose way, I imagine that God is trying to tell me that nature is bigger than I am, that beauty will eventually win out over shit. That the sun will come up and go down despite every lousy fucked-up thing that happens on this earth. It doesn't sniff out signs of impending trouble and evacuate like I do. It departs graciously, with color and light, intermingling with shadows that contribute their own muted beauty to the scene. It always leaves and it always returns. I need to burn that into my brain.

It is hard to leave the beach. I wait for a long time after sunset, till every bit of yellow is gone and the sky is pale pink, far off in the distance. Everything around me is quiet. People speak in hushed tones. Kites come down. Children are gathered up for bed. We allow the day to come to a close.

I am tremendously reassured by what I see. Somehow it helps me to believe that I will be alright. Maybe not great. But alright.

August 4, 1991

I turn the words over in my mind and on my tongue. "My grandmother is dead." I try to make it make sense. I say she was old. I say she lived a good life. I say she died a good death. I say all the stupid things I swore I'd never say about anyone I loved.

The letter I wrote to her two weeks ago sits on the hall table, begging for a stamp. One lousy twenty-nine-cent stamp. Thirty seconds to rifle through my purse. A five-minute trip to the post office. I open the letter and read the sanitized version of my life, knowing that my grandmother needed my news and not my blues. The two beers I swallow as I move in my rocking chair help me to stop making sense and finally allow myself the luxury of tears.

My brother Chip borrows a van and we drive all night to Boston. We admire the wealth of snacks supplied by Priscilla, the junk-food connoisseur, and polish off a box of Ho-Ho's before we even hit 95. Reliving old rivalries, we argue about who took the most.

I take a wrong turn coming out of a rest-stop bathroom. I don't have my glasses on and wander up and down rows of parked cars in the dark. I can't remember the color or make of the van. Finally, I find it. But when I open the door and try to climb in, the family from Montreal does not look at all pleased to see me. I have no money. I can't see a thing and I look like

I've slept in my clothes, which I have. I hear Chip calling my name. He sounds really annoyed. For ten minutes I listen to my siblings complain that I can really be an airhead, that I pee too much, and that I snore. I concede the peeing and airhead points but hotly deny the snoring.

In the darkness and the motion, I have a dream or a memory. I'll never know which.

I am sailing alone. My grandmother is waving to me from the house. She is worried for my safety, knowing that I have no sense of the wind and will end, as always, overturned in the water. She is waving me in, calling to me to come in closer. But I pretend she is just waving hello, and I wave back. For once in my life, I make friends with the wind and fly across the ocean. Away from shore. Away from her. I sail away and hope that somehow she will understand.

August 5, 1991

We fall silent when we unlock her door and enter her house, each of us lonely in the memories of other arrivals. The creaking of the big blue door, the loud ticking of the grandfather clock in the hall. Calling, "Grandmother, Grandmother. We're here. We're finally here." The endless hugs, the light in her eyes. We wander her halls, climb her stairs, caress her things. Silently, reverently, already mourning the welcome we will never know again.

My father, Chip, and I go shopping for the reception after the funeral. At the paper-goods store, the combination of too little sleep and too much caffeine catches up with us. I insist on the Boston Celtics paper plates, knowing how crazy she was about her teams. Chip prefers a Hawaiian motif and holds up an aloha banner. We banter back and forth about whether *aloha* means hello or good-bye. My father interrupts to inform us that, so far, we have been absolutely no help. I try to straighten up but collapse again into laughter when thirty-seven-year-old Chip asks, "Dad, does this mean you won't buy us ice cream cones on the way home?"

We progress to the grocery store. As she scans our groceries at the checkout, the perky cashier comments, "Someone's having a really big party."

My silliness is replaced by irritation. The third time she says it, I answer, "Actually, someone's having a really big funeral." That shuts her right up. I feel like a bitch, but I don't care.

My mother takes me aside and tells me that the silver my grandmother promised me was also promised to my cousin Paula. I act like a hurt child and whine, "But she promised!"

"Your grandmother made a lot of promises that she didn't keep," my mother responds gently.

I tiptoe upstairs to where Brian is napping, sit down next to him, and stare at him really hard, willing him to awaken. When he stirs, I feign surprise, like I had no intention of waking him. Before his eyes are fully open, I spill out the whole story. Brian rubs the sleep from his eyes and growls, "Screw the silver." As he pulls me down toward him, I try to remember that sex is almost always better than sympathy, and let him silence me with kisses.

At the funeral home, I brace myself for the sickening smell of funeral flowers. I approach the casket to see my grandmother. I study her hands, noticing how different they look. Why couldn't they have left a little paint under her fingernails and my grandfather's clunky gold watch on her wrist?

Keara hangs back at the door. I go to her and gently, but firmly, tell her that there is nothing to fear. Instantly I realize that I have just uttered what my grandmother would call a "boldfaced lie." I admit to Keara, and to myself, that this is scary as hell and encourage her to sit in the adjoining room for as long as she wants.

The room is packed with mourners. I take a breather and sit down with my sister Rachel. As Chip walks toward us, we both notice that he has just hiked up his pants and walked exactly like our father. We look at each other and laugh so hard that people turn to stare. Neither of us can stop laughing, so I put my arm around her and wipe my eyes so that people will think we're really crying.

Sarah arrives from New Jersey. We have been estranged for so long because of too much alcohol on her part, and too little compassion on mine. We grab a couch in a quiet corner. She tells me about her recovery and her involvement in AA. As we talk, I realize that she is nowhere near taking each day at a time but is surviving minute by minute, an experience I know well. We talk about pain. We talk about God. She tells me that in AA they say that religion is for people who are afraid of going to hell. Spirituality is for people who have already been there. I say, "Amen," and squeeze her hand, knowing that for the first time in years we understand each other. She tries to find the location of the closest AA meeting. When the timing doesn't work, I suggest that there are enough people in the family to make a sizable meeting. I count off the alcoholic relatives on my fingers, using both hands.

I shake hands with every octogenarian in the local art association. I kiss people I don't remember. I am incredibly polite to people I've never liked. I tell people that my life is going a lot better than it really is.

August 6, 1991

It is 2:00 A.M. and I can't sleep. I pull out my grandmother's photograph albums. Her whole life is condensed into
images on pages. I see my mother as a child. I see myself. It is
my first birthday. I am brown with the sun. My hair is white. I
am round and happy. I slip the picture out of the album and
turn it over. On the back of the picture in my grandmother's
handwriting are the words *My golden girl.* When did I stop
being golden? Can I ever get it back again?

Her bottle of antidepressants is next to her bed. I take it
to my brother Mark and tell him that since we both inherited
the curse, we both, by rights, deserve the cure. He tells me that
I'm twisted, but holds out his hand to take his share.

As I'm dressing for the funeral, my mother calls me to my
grandmother's room. Her hands are full of rosary beads—all
kinds, some broken, most intact. They range in color, quality,
and texture, from glass beads cut like diamonds attached with
silver, to a tiny set of blue plastic beads on a piece of string. My
grandmother collected these beads on her trips to cathedrals
and shrines. Some even have microscopic relics of saints or
chapels encased in plastic. My mother asks if I want them. I am
surprised. I've never told her of the nights when I used strings
of beads to ward off the voices in my head that commanded me
to let go, to give up. She places them in my hands and says, "I'm
sorry about the silver. We'll work something out." I accept the
beads from my mother, realizing that it doesn't much matter to
me who gets what. My grandmother only entertained with the
silver. She held on for dear life with these beads.

We return to the funeral home before mass. Each person in the family approaches the casket to say good-bye. My
brother and cousin kneel and bless themselves in synchrony. I

can almost feel my breathing change with theirs. Their shoulders rise and fall, heaving and crying. My mother and my aunt bend into them and hold them. Keara wrestles with her fears and finally approaches the casket. I can see the memory in her eyes as she registers her grief and cries in my arms.

I walk to the lectern on the altar to give the first reading at the funeral mass. It is from Lamentations. I read the beginning words:

> My soul is deprived of peace.
> I have forgotten what happiness is.
> I tell myself that my future is lost . . .

The words swim on the page. A pain moves down my chest like a fault line. I feel myself merge with my grandmother and doubt my ability to continue. "Breathe," I tell myself. "Keep going." "Finish." When I return to my seat, my uncle puts his hands on my shoulders and whispers, "I'm proud to know you."

At the cemetery we answer the prayers of the priest as he gives the final commendation. People drift away to their cars. The great-grandchildren play with the flowers on the grave. They make small bouquets. They dance and run. I hear echoes of my grandfather, resting in the same ground. In his pretend-gruff voice, he yells, "Hey, you kids, get off this grave."

Then I smile for a moment at the sound of my grandmother answering, "Hush, Harry. They're fine just where they are."

Back at the house we assemble on the porch for family pictures. A cousin finds an old picture of all twenty grandchildren surrounding my grandmother. We decide to re-create it and agree to assume the position and demeanor we had in the picture. It takes at least ten minutes to get organized. I strike the pose of the oldest grandchild, sullen and bored at the age of fourteen. A thirty-year-old cardiologist stands next to me with his finger up his nose. A twenty-eight-year-old BMW salesman pokes a thirty-two-year-old CPA in the ribs. I laugh harder than I have in a long time.

We linger after pictures because no one wants to break the mood. We plead with my uncle to play the piano so that we can sing some of the songs that he's written over the years. We teach the songs to the great-grandchildren. When we run out of songs that everyone knows, we resort to Christmas carols, even though the summer heat is pushing ninety degrees. The great-grandchildren stand in a line and sing "So Long, Farewell" from *The Sound of Music.* They each take a turn, twirl around, and disappear as we sing good-bye.

In a burst, in an instant, I realize that here in this room is the best of who I am. In this room is the memory of who I was and the promise of who I still can be. It is wit and hope and blind tenacity. It is touching and loving and holding on. It is my grandmother's gift to my mother, my mother's gift to me, and my gift to Keara.

I forgive my mother for being so strong. I forgive my grandmother for not being strong enough. I try to forgive myself for being both.

We say our reluctant good-byes and pile into the van for the long drive home. We drive down her street one last time. I take it all in, every house, lamppost, and shrub. As we turn off her street, I close my eyes. In the darkness and the motion, I see my grandmother again.

We are at the beach house. She is waving to me as I sail into shore. As I get closer, she moves farther away. I motion for her to come back, but she only waves, as if to greet me. I scream for her to return to me, but she doesn't listen. Then I realize that it is she who is sailing away. Farther and farther. Until she is small. Until she is gone. Until she is only a memory.

August 10, 1991

A six-year-old named Ben is referred to me. He is preoccupied with his infant brother, Stephen, who died six months ago. His parents are concerned because initially he seemed to be the one who responded the "best" to the death, which in our culture often means that he responded the "least."

Ben is a freckle-faced redhead dressed in a baseball shirt and jeans. He looks like the kind of kid who is probably harboring a member of the reptile family in one of his pockets. When I ask him what's on his mind, he tells me that he is "sad" because he can't stop thinking about his brother. I ask him how he pictures Stephen now.

He answers, "Mom and Dad think he's in heaven with all the other kids that got dead." He gets very quiet and stares at the floor. I let the silence surround us for a while and he adds, "But I don't know about God and heaven. I can't see it in my head."

"So Mom and Dad's picture doesn't help you like it helps them," I suggest.

He looks ashamed and answers, "No." We are both quiet for several moments and I feel an aching sadness fill up the space between us. With wide eyes and a confidential whisper he tells me, "Some people think that when you die you come back as other things."

"Really?" I ask. "Like what?"

"Like animals and trees and flowers and stuff like that." He smiles as he says it, but then instantly pulls back and insists, "But, of course, I don't believe that!"

I smile mischievously and prod him, "Yeah, but if you did, what would you come back as?"

"I'd come back as a blue jay . . . because I like the bird . . . and I like the team."

"And Mom?" I ask. "What would she come back as?"

"A cardinal . . . and Dad would be an eagle . . . a bald one." We laugh. Things get quiet again.

"And Stephen?" I ask softly. "What would Stephen be?"

He thinks for a moment and replies, "Stephen would be the water that we all drink from."

"The water? Like in a birdbath?" I ask.

"Yeah, but not just a birdbath. That would run out. Like the water in all the creeks and all the rivers and all the oceans. And the birds could drink from it and never run out . . . not never. . . . Stephen could be the water."

The sorrow on Ben's face turns to pleasure at the image he has created. I don't know what my face looks like, but I know that this kid has just blown me away. Sometimes in my work I have the clear sense that the direction in which money usually changes hands should be reversed, and I should pay them. This is one of those times.

September 15, 1991

Each time I feel myself slowing down, losing vitality and strength, I am terrified that I will be drawn like a magnet back down those dark stairs and long halls to that awful time and place and self. I am still having smaller depressions that typically respond to simple alterations in medication. I have good days and bad days. Really shitty things happen. I cry and curse in sadness, pain, and frustration. I get so mad I want to throw things. I get discouraged and demoralized. But it's not depression. It doesn't even come close.

I'm sitting on the sidelines of this weekend with pneumonia. My chest feels like it's been kicked. In the week before I knew I was sick, I started to drag and became afraid. The record on the stereo started getting slower and slower in its revolutions. Color turned to gray. My energy failed me. I was sure I was back on the road to hell. When I finally took my temperature and the thermometer registered 101 degrees, I said, "Thank God." The doctor frowned as he listened to my lungs and winced as I coughed my guts out. But I was delighted with the diagnosis in a way that no one else could understand.

I am exhausted and short of breath. I have to sleep straight up in bed. Each cough feels like it registers a seven on the Richter scale. But I am essentially alright.

Whenever anything lousy happens and I begin to feel sorry for myself, I ask, "Is this worse than depression?" And when the answer is no, then I tell myself, "Shut up." It's not that I lack compassion for my difficulties. It's just that my baseline for awful will never be the same. After you've been through an earthquake, those ruts in the road will never feel quite as deep.

September 20, 1991

We're having both families over for dinner. Keara's job for the morning is to clean out the downstairs medicine cabinet. It is crammed with bottles, a graveyard of pills and potions I tried over the past year. Keara wipes out the cabinet by sweeping the bottles off the shelves and collecting them all on a silver hors d'oeuvre tray I've just polished for the party.

Ginger stops by for a minute and we check in with each other over tea in the living room. I yell in to Keara, "How's it going in there?" She appears with the pill bottles heaped on the silver tray. With a flourish, she bends over and extends the tray to us, "Mints?" she offers innocently. "Nuts? Antidepressants?"

October 1, 1991

It is a crackling fall day, the morning bursting apart with color and cold. The transition to autumn is difficult for me this year. With the end of summer, I feel myself casting shadows that grow longer with each day. They follow me and loom large and threatening. I feel it in the chill in the air, the yellow mums on porch steps, the piles of pumpkins on street corners, the dressing of the trees. It grows in my body from an itch to an ache, to a deep-down wrenching pain.

The therapist in me knows intellectually that this is an anniversary reaction to my hospitalization last fall. But knowledge is so different from experience. I thought anniversary reactions meant being tuned into the calendar on the wall. You notice a date and think, "Oh no, at this time last year that bad thing happened." Then you feel the grief and the pain. But that's not it at all. Your memory isn't in the calendar. It's in your bones. Your body remembers what your mind forgets.

The images are visual, auditory, olfactory, kinesthetic. They aren't laid down on the same tracks as thought. And sometimes when they return to you, it is as if you feel them for the very first time. Memory lives on in the details, like the color of a room, the tone of a voice, the touch of a child, the smell of a man.

October 31, 1991

One year ago today I had my final ECT treatment and was released from the hospital. I have struggled greatly over this year with the shame of the depression, the hospital, the ECT. I've seen them as concrete signs of giving up, falling apart, getting an "F" in life. Being hospitalized on a psychiatric unit was, for me, like crossing over into a different state. I've lost citizenship in the old place, but I haven't totally settled into the new one either. There has been a loss of innocence in it all. Some reckoning, in a real live showdown, of my own vulnerability, my capacity for unraveling, the limits of my effort and will. It is knowing that I am capable of falling, that I am fragile. That life can spin out of control for anyone is something I should have known from my work with patients. But to actually feel myself in the skid is entirely different from intellectual knowledge. To know the force of the avalanche and my powerlessness over it is to feel myself in brand-new territory.

In choosing the hospital and ECT I chose to fight for my life. Despite the continuing cycle of disquieting ups and downs, I am living the life I fought for. I know it in the joy of an ice-cold Diet Coke in a plastic cup, the fluidity of motion in swimming laps, the soft touch of Keara's breasts against mine as she seeks the same refuge she has for thirteen years. It is in the sound of my own laughter, the stirring between my legs as I feel the old wanting, the capacity to read, to watch, to follow, to listen.

For so long now I have waited to get back to baseline and return to exactly the same point from which I originally set out on these travels. My criterion for healing has been to be able to pick up right where I left off, like midpage in a novel. I have waited and waited, but I'm still not back to that page. Kay and Lew try to tell me, in their own gentle ways, to stop waiting. I think they're trying to tell me that I'm never going to get back to that page. That I'm in an entirely new book now, most of it unwritten.

A messenger delivers a package from Kay. It is a book called *Hymns and Fragments* by the German poet Friedrich Hölderlin. Inside the cover she has inscribed simply, "Congratulations." I sit down on the floor and read it. Hölderlin's writing reflects both the desolation and the exultation of his "madness." The last poem, "In Lovely Blue," makes me weep and brings back so many of the talks Kay and I have had over the past year. I read one passage again and again:

> A grave spirit arises from within,
> Out of divers things. Yet so simple
> These images, so very holy,
> One fears to describe them. But the gods,
> Ever kind in all things,
> Are rich in virtue and joy.
> Which man may imitate.
> May a man look up
> From the utter hardship of his life
> And say: Let me also be
> Like these? Yes. As long as kindness lasts,
> Pure within his heart, he may gladly measure himself
> Against the divine.

November 5, 1991

Whenever we drive by the hospital, which we do all the time, I wonder if Keara ever thinks about it like I do. She has never been real big on "processing" things in those introspective, reflective ways that make psychologists happy. Keara does not hold a lot of stock in the value of talking about your feelings on a subject that's already a done deal.

When her goldfish died (actually, when I accidentally killed them), she was visibly upset when I told her. She put her head down and cried, "Oh no, they were the closest things I'll ever have to pets." I asked her if she'd like to talk about it. She looked at me like I'd just suggested we pick our noses and asked challengingly, "Why?" When I stammered and told her that sometimes it makes people feel better, she just looked at me and insisted, again, "Why?" daring me to give some kind of sensible answer. What could I say? People pay me big bucks every day just to talk to me about how they feel. But it makes absolutely no sense to my own child, who can get it for free.

When Mr. Hooper died on *Sesame Street,* Big Bird started crying and talking about his grief. Keara stood up in disgust, put her hands over her ears, and screamed, "*Sesame Street* is a stupid baby show and I am never watching it again." She ran into her room and turned up her tinny Fisher-Price record player full blast while Brian and I sniffled our way through Mr. Hooper's memorial. I've learned over the years that the frontal approach doesn't work with this kid. Neither does anything remotely resembling what she calls "shrink talk."

Still, I wonder how all of this has been for her. But she never talks about it. On our way to her friend Phoebe's, we pass the hospital. We lapse into silence. I am lost in my memories. I have no idea where she is.

She says casually, "Jennifer seems to be doing pretty well."

I'm thinking, "Who the hell is Jennifer?" and then realize that she's talking about my roommate on the psych unit. I feel like I am tiptoeing around a land mine with her. I don't want to do anything to scare her away from the first window of opportunity to actually talk about this.

I ask her how she can tell that Jennifer is doing well. She describes seeing her laughing with her friends and hanging out with her boyfriend. Keara tells me, "She looked beautiful and happy."

Several moments go by. We pass the hospital. She asks if Jennifer had ECT, if I think Jennifer takes medicine. I say that I honestly don't know. She looks perplexed and asks, "Mom, why do these things happen? Everything seemed okay."

I can't tell whether she's talking about Jennifer or me. I start in on a treatise about the psychological and biological theories of depression, but she begins fiddling with the radio dials and I can tell I'm losing her. So I settle on the truth. My voice is full of tears.

I say, "I don't know, baby. I used to think I knew. But I was wrong."

"Well, I think Jennifer is a lot better," she says with resolution.

"I am so glad," I tell her.

We drive a ways without talking, with only the radio music between us. There is something hanging in the air, waiting to be said. We turn the corner into the cul-de-sac where Phoebe lives. Keara turns to me and tries to say very casually, "I think I'm much more like Dad's side of the family, don't you?"

I want to tell her that each day I see in her some glittering threads of my own family, woven through the generations. I want to tell her how those golden strands are as much a part of our legacy as the darkness. But I look at my sweet red-haired child for whom I would go through one hundred depressions to spare her just one, and know that it is not, right now, what she needs to hear.

"Yeah, sweetie," I answer, leaning over and stroking her cheek. "You're much more like Dad's side."

She plants a quick satisfied kiss on my cheek and slams the car door. As she dances up the steps, she turns to look at me one more time. I smile back at her and wave good-bye. She disappears behind the big green door and I utter a silent prayer that she's right.

November 10, 1991

When I arrive at the monastery, it's like coming home. There is an image that comes to me as I pull off Route 7 onto the gravel road that leads to the abbey. In my fantasy, loved ones run out to meet me, to embrace me, on my return home. No one, of course, is ever there. It's the place itself that greets me. I set down my bags and search out Brother Francis, who gives me a hug and asks, "You been doin' okay?" Other than him and Brother Joseph at the gift cottage, I don't know a soul.

When I am here, I remember arriving at my grand-mother's house as a child. After a ten-hour drive, I had to run to each room in her sprawling house, all four floors, surveying them, vigilant for changes, seeking security in the sameness of their sights and smells. Assured that it was all still there, I could take my place again with my family, and stand in the long line for Grandmother's individualized loving and effusive welcomes. Here at the monastery I run to check out my room, the small desk with the bronze crucifix, the thin bed, the long windows framing the Blue Ridge Mountains, the abbey chapel, the pond, the broad oak tree with the same stone bench. Yes. It's all here. It's all the same. I can stop looking now. Put the inventory away. I am home.

Vespers begin as they always do, with the ringing of the bell. The monks chant, "O Lord, come to my assistance. Make haste to help me." The first reading is from Psalm 56. It is read by an old monk, stooped over and slow. He fumbles with the page. But his voice is vibrant and strong.

> You have kept an account of my wanderings;
> You have kept a record of my tears;
> Are they not written in your book?

For you rescued my soul from death,
you kept my feet from stumbling,
That I may walk in the presence of God
and enjoy the light of the living.

I struggle to keep from losing it. I am so moved by the words. Then the second reading: the story of Martha and Mary. Jesus says, "Martha, Martha, you are anxious and troubled about many things. . . ." I feel self-conscious, even though I am totally alone in the back row. It seems like this is about as close as God gets to Fed-Exing a message to a person. I remember the priest, the one who told me that "someday" I would "understand." The words would "explode" in my head, and my life would "never be the same." It's safe to say that he hit the jackpot on that prediction. I think someday has come. I think a number of things have exploded in my head. And as much as I've been trying to the contrary, I realize now that my life will never be the same again.

Retreat Day Two

On a long walk I stop to study the cows who always make me laugh in their absolute and total indifference. I take a nap in my sweats, with my running shoes still on. When I wake up, the afternoon sun is blessing me from the long window in my room. I move the chair in front of the window and sit in the light and the warmth. The sun is so strong on my face it's hard to believe there is a windowpane between us. I eat an orange that I brought from home. Not in the usual way I inhale food, but in slow motion. I love feeling it and smelling it and watching the tiny bursts of spray as I peel it. I decide that oranges like this are meant less to be eaten than to be received. I eat it slice by slice as I cook in the sun, moving like a cat in the chair to keep the sun on my face as it shifts.

At dinner Brother Francis reads to us. He drags a little school desk into the dining room, pours himself a small glass of juice, and situates his long body in the seat. The deep sleeves of his robe are rolled up to his elbows, his heavy work boots stick out under the folds. He surveys the room for readiness, then reaches into his robe and pulls out a small book. It is a collection of stories by a priest, Edward Hays. He first reads from the back cover about the healing power of stories and how at different points in history and cultures, stories were prescribed for people who were "sick at heart." I remember all the poems Kay gave me as part of my own healing.

Francis settles back and reads a story about the chess pieces on a chessboard and why they all smile. It is about a king who "lost today." His bishop takes him to the past (yesterday) and his knights and queen take him to the future (tomorrow). But he keeps wanting to know who stole "today." He finally finds today and tries to celebrate it with his people. As the celebration progresses, someone gets nervous and asks, "What time is it?" to which the king answers, "Now." Another person asks anxiously, "Where are we?" to which he replies serenely, "Here."

I guess I've held a stereotype of monks as social isolates, a self-selected group who couldn't, or didn't want to, interact with others. The monks I've seen are gracious and joyful. Not in that born-again proselytizing way that makes me want to retch, but in a simple, very real way. They aren't as disconnected from life as I expected. They know music and slang. They are well read and open to a great variety of ways of accessing the divine. I think my stereotype served a purpose—I could only imagine someone choosing this kind of life because of a defect in his character. But one must really be tremendously strong to live this kind of life.

The other thought that comes to me is that we all have to commit to some degree of solitude and reflection in our lives. While my life does not have the built-in ease of the quiet and aloneness that I find here, I am responsible for finding some. It is my choice. I need the quiet reflection more than I ever knew before.

I find myself growing quieter over time. But I'm so unused to it that I still equate it with being overwhelmed or depressed—a default in the continual cycle of inundation and backing off. And yet the quiet is part of who I am. Not just a result of the circuits blowing and the computer shutting down. It has merit all by itself.

Retreat Day Three

I sit in my sunny spot by the window, reading from the best known of the Trappist monks, Thomas Merton. He writes about his own experience of illness: "Sometimes a call to spiritual solitude and liberty may come to us masked as a humiliating sickness or weakness." Yes, Thomas. You've got that one right.

Sometimes lately, even though I am not depressed, sadness rushes in and fills up every space in me like a wave washes through a sand castle. Even when the wave recedes, it leaves behind a sea reservoir, and the castle will never be the same. The past two years have challenged so many assumptions I held about myself. Sand castles I had spent a lot of time planning and building fell hard with a couple of big waves. I was really attached to those castles. I worked hard to build them, and when they were dashed, I felt like I'd been left with nothing. I had worked so hard to create the foundations of a good life. I worked hard and I worked fast, always trying to accomplish more than one thing at a time. Going to college and getting married, having a baby while getting a doctorate, moving my husband and toddler five hundred miles to a Harvard post-doctoral fellowship, just to enhance my curriculum vitae. I thought achievement was the express route to happiness and that competence guaranteed contentment. I erected a monument to industry and effort. But I had no idea it was made only of sand.

When the career in academics was not as bright as I had hoped, a castle crumbled. When my work as a therapist became unsatisfying and draining, a castle crumbled. When I lost the babies I'd always assumed that I would have, a castle crumbled.

So I rebuilt, always trying to copy the first castles. I was sure that since the first ones fell, I was entitled to have the next ones stand. But that wasn't true. The new ones toppled over with other waves. I tried to say, "What the hell. That's life. I can take it." But I was wrong.

There is no getting away from a wave that's got your name on it. The tide will come in whether you want it to or not. And there really isn't a damn thing you can do to stop it, reverse it, or even delay it. Forget it. You have to plant your feet solidly in the sand and get yourself anchored. And then you have to ready yourself to take a couple of direct hits from the water. You loosen your body and you move with each wave. You get salt in your nose and mouth, and the ocean rakes sand and stones over your feet and legs. Your eyes sting, and you feel so tired. But there is really nothing else to do.

The tide will come and go. The sun will be warm again, and the salt on your skin will remind you of what you have done. And you will rest your tired body on the shore, falling into that delicious sleep that comes from knowing you are alright.

Retreat Day Four

I spend the early morning in the retreat library. On a little cassette recorder I listen to the lectures that Thomas Merton gave to the novices at his monastery. Even though they have deadly titles like "The Desert Fathers," they are lively, witty, and informative. I wander around the library, perusing the books and delighting in these monks who blend what I know to be basic Catholicism, mysticism, and radical social action.

There is a book about the saints, and I look up my old friend St. Martha, frowning when I see her listed as the patroness of housewives, domestics, and waitresses. But as I read more about her, I realize my mother was right. She did get a raw deal in the Bible. With many of the early saints, you don't hear too much follow-up about them after the death of Christ. But legend has it that Martha, along with her resilient brother Lazarus and contemplative sister Mary, escaped to Provence. The town was said to be terrorized by a dragon. Unlike so many of the heroes of the day who subdued monsters and dragons by beating the crap out of them, Martha took a different approach. She sprinkled the dragon's tail with holy water, tied her silken belt around it, and led it peacefully from the town. There is something in that legend that moves me deeply.

My friend Ginger always teases me that I go after everything in my life like I'm "fighting snakes." St. Martha saved the town from its terror, not by charging ahead with that kind of force and will, but by allying herself with the thing that she most feared. She gave the object of her fear something that it needed and wanted. And in that way, she saved them both. While I don't qualify as a housewife, domestic, or waitress, this woman still has much to teach me. I have come to some fragile peace with the trials of the past years. But the peace only works when I think of depression in the safe and distant "past." The terror of possible depression in the "future" haunts me daily. I hate that dragon. It is my enemy. I am vigilant for it, scrambling to find out how I can prevent it from returning. Or, failing that, how I can assault the hell out of it if it returns. But St. Martha's story illuminates an entirely different way of thinking about that thing which I fear so intensely.

I remember one of my favorite passages from Rilke's *Letters to a Young Poet*. His writing about suffering and fear has always consoled me to the point that I have whole passages committed to memory. But now, echoes of a different passage come to me. One that had always left me puzzled and unsettled, but now allows me the deepest of comforts:

> How should we be able to forget those ancient myths that are at the beginning of all peoples, the myths about dragons that at the last moment turn into princesses; perhaps all the dragons of our lives are princesses who are only waiting to see us once beautiful and brave. Perhaps everything terrible is in its deepest being something helpless that wants help from us.

Retreat Day Five

In packing my clothes I notice that I have basically lived in the same sweat suit all four days. I look like hell. But I feel like heaven. Brother Francis gives me a huge hug and walks me to my car. I fight the urge to beg, "Just let me stay here a few more days." On the way out, I stop at the gift cottage to say good-bye to Brother Joseph. I gaze longingly at the rows of preserves—wicked wonderful ones like black raspberry with liqueur. I try to think of people who would like them. But then I own up to the fact that it is I who would like them and, diet or no diet, it is I who will have them. I buy a jar of raspberry and a jar of peach. As I'm leaving, Brother Joseph points out loaves of bread that have just been carried in from the bakery out back. They are so warm that the steam is still visible on the outside of the plastic bags. I buy a loaf of white and a loaf of whole wheat.

Driving down the long snowy driveway that crackles with ice, rocks, and twigs all the way down, I say out loud to no one, "Good-bye, good-bye. I'll be back soon. And soon after that. . . ."

Out on Route 7 I begin to smell the bread. The fresh yeastiness of it is too much for me. The impulse control I struggle so hard to maintain succumbs in one second to the pleasures of the flesh. I can't find anything to use to spread the wicked jam on the freshly baked bread. So I pull over to the side of the road. I open the jar of peach preserves, stick my fingers down deep in the jar, and slap the jam on the bread. Before I can eat the bread, I have to clean my hands. I can't find anything for cleaning. So I lick each finger, carefully, to get everything. The bread goes down fast. Then come the inevitable empirical questions about which jam will taste best on which bread. I pull over too many times and eat too many bread-and-jam and finger sandwiches. But I can honestly say that the ride home, with all its bread and jam and licking and dripping, is one of the happiest moments I have known. Ever.

ACKNOWLEDGMENTS

When a person writes about herself, it is difficult to differentiate the people who helped her with her life from the people who helped her with her book. In my case, there is considerable overlap.

The generosity and constancy of my parents, John and Mary Louise Manning, are a great gift. They provided me with a family in which I learned that difficulty can always be tempered with humor. My brothers and sisters, Chip, Sarah, Priscilla, Mark, and Rachel, often a major source of irritation in my childhood, are now a major source of pleasure. Whenever I am in danger of taking myself too seriously, ten minutes with one of my siblings will bring me right back down to earth. The addition of the "outlaws," Ann, Greg, and the memory of Darrell, has been the icing on the family cake. My mother-in-law, Jane Depenbrock, has contributed her enthusiasm and support throughout this project. Through my uncle, David Cooney, I learned to follow my imagination and never to be afraid of coloring outside the lines.

Patricia Dalton, Ginger Hays, and Louise Swanberg have taught me so much about the friendships I describe in this story. Ed Sharp has provided his companionship, his humor, and his patient computer assistance to a person so computer illiterate that she can't even pronounce MS-DOS correctly. "Women's Group"—Margaret, Peggy, Lynne, Marcia, Jenny, Ginger, and Nelly—encircles me with love and serve as a constant reminder of the wonder of women's oral traditions.

The Hall family and the monks at the Holy Cross Abbey provided quiet havens in which I could escape the chaos of my study and contemplate this book in blissful order and silence.

I will be forever grateful to Lew Bigelow, Kay Redfield Jamison, Jeremy Waletzky, and Thomas Jacob for their technical expertise, their gentle kindness, and their belief that I would always prevail.

Rich Simon's response to my early work was the best shot in the arm a fledgling writer could get. He is responsible for encouraging me to consider expanding the piece that originally appeared in *The Family Therapy Networker* into this full-length book.

Working with my editor, Barbara Moulton, has been pure magic. I appreciate her vision, her wit, and her remediation of years of grammatical indifference.

My agents, Arielle Eckstut and James Levine of James Levine Communications, Inc., contributed energy, enthusiasm, and a contagious belief in the viability of this project.

I am grateful to my patients, who teach me on a daily basis what it means both to suffer and to savor these lives we are given.

My daughter, Keara, blesses each morning with her exuberant shower songs. In the dark times, they have been my sustenance. In the light times, they are one of the greatest joys a mother can know.

And finally, I give thanks to my husband, Brian, who has believed in my writing since he received my first love letter at the age of sixteen. He has kept the dream alive during the hardest of times, when I was unable to sleep, let alone to dream. He will always be the truest of loves, the most trusted of critics, and the funniest damn person I have ever known.